CONTENTS

Introduction

Dino Fun

Meat Eaters

Plant Eaters

Sea and Sky

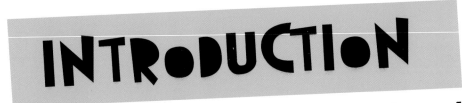

INTRODUCTION

Get ready for some fearsome folding as we explore the world of dinosaur origami. You'll learn how to make everything from Triceratops to T. rex, and even create your own set of dino claws!

A lot of the origami models in this book are made with the same folds and basic designs, known as "bases." This introduction explains some of the ones that will appear most, so it's a good idea to master these folds and bases before you start. When making the projects, follow the key below to find out what the lines and arrows mean.

KEY

- - - - - valley fold

•••••• mountain fold

✂ cut with scissors

◀ push

⟲ rotate

↷ direction to move paper

↻ turn paper over

⟋ apply glue

⚡ step fold

VALLEY FOLD

To make a valley fold, fold the paper toward you, so that the crease is pointing away from you, like a valley.

MOUNTAIN FOLD

To make a mountain fold, fold the paper so that the crease is pointing up toward you, like a mountain.

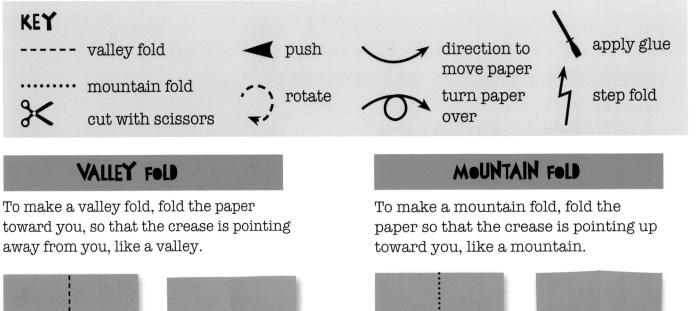

STEP FOLD

A step fold is used to make a zigzag in the paper. We'll use it to make ears, tails, and other dino features.

 1 Valley fold the paper in half. Then make a mountain fold directly above the valley fold.

 2 Push the mountain fold down over the valley fold and press down flat.

 3 You now have a step fold. You can also make it in reverse, with the mountain fold first.

 4

INSIDE REVERSE FOLD

This is a useful fold if you want to flatten part of an origami model. It's a good way to create tails and snouts for your dinosaurs.

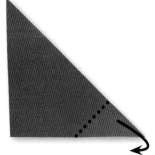

1 Fold a piece of paper diagonally in half. Make a valley fold on one corner and crease.

2 It's important to make sure that the paper is creased well. Run your finger over the crease two or three times.

3 Refold the crease you just made into a mountain fold, then unfold. Open up the corner slightly.

4 Open up the paper a little more and then tuck the tip of the corner inside. Close the paper. This is the view from the underside of the paper.

5 Flatten the paper. You now have an inside reverse fold.

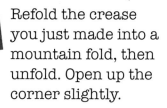

OUTSIDE REVERSE FOLD

This is great if you want to make part of your model stick out. It will come in handy for making heads and crests.

1 Fold a piece of paper diagonally in half. Make a valley fold on one corner and crease.

2 It's important to make sure that the paper is creased well. Run your finger over the crease two or three times.

3 Refold the crease you just made into a mountain fold, then unfold. Open up the corner slightly.

4 Open up the paper a little more and start to turn the corner inside out. Then close the paper when the fold begins to turn.

5 You now have an outside reverse fold. You can either flatten the paper or leave it rounded out.

KITE BASE

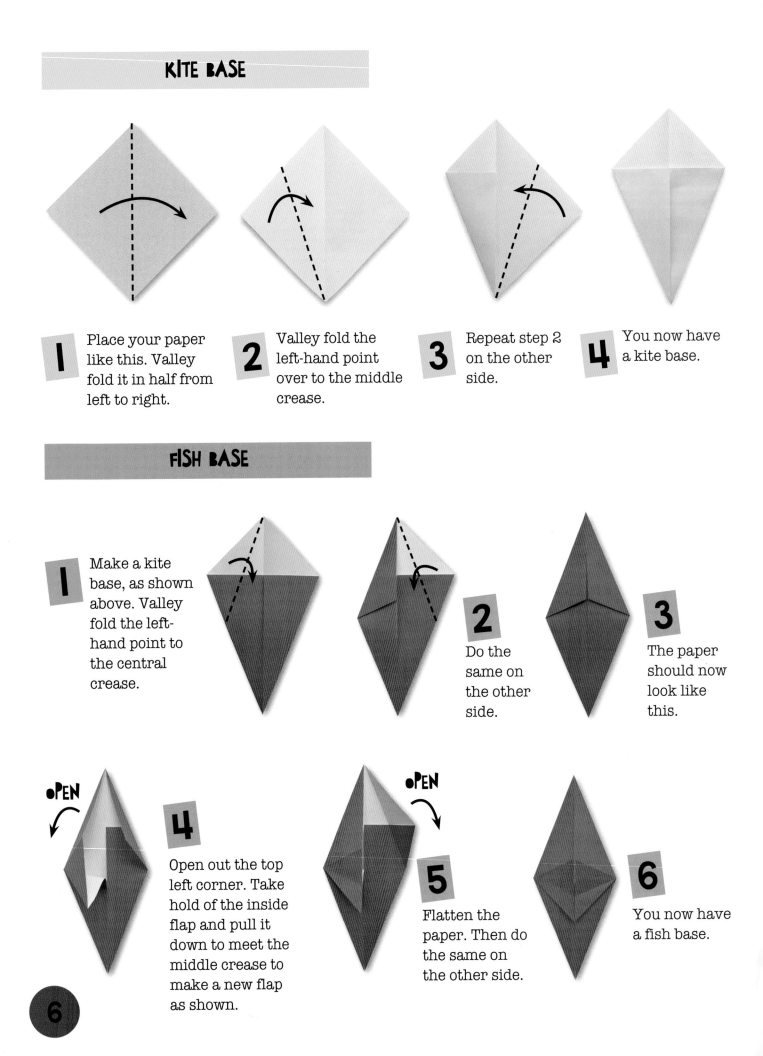

1 Place your paper like this. Valley fold it in half from left to right.

2 Valley fold the left-hand point over to the middle crease.

3 Repeat step 2 on the other side.

4 You now have a kite base.

FISH BASE

1 Make a kite base, as shown above. Valley fold the left-hand point to the central crease.

2 Do the same on the other side.

3 The paper should now look like this.

OPEN

4 Open out the top left corner. Take hold of the inside flap and pull it down to meet the middle crease to make a new flap as shown.

OPEN

5 Flatten the paper. Then do the same on the other side.

6 You now have a fish base.

6

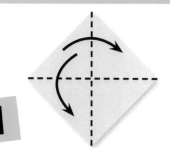

TURN OVER

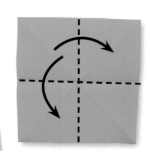

1 Make a fold from top to bottom and unfold. Then make a fold from left to right and unfold.

2 Turn your paper over and rotate it so that one side is facing you.

3 Fold from top to bottom and unfold. Then fold from left to right and unfold.

PUSH ► ◄ **PUSH**

4 Push the paper into this shape, so the middle point pops up.

5 Push the sides in, bringing the back and front sections together.

6 Flatten the paper. You now have a waterbomb base.

TURN OVER

1 Fold from top to bottom and unfold. Then fold from left to right and unfold.

2 Turn your paper over and rotate it so that one side is facing you.

3 Valley fold along the horizontal and vertical lines and unfold.

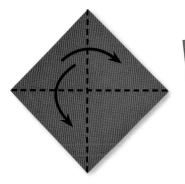

PUSH ► ◄ **PUSH**

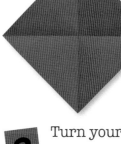

4 Rotate the paper so a corner is facing you.

5 Hold the paper by opposite diagonal corners. Push the two corners together so that the shape begins to collapse.

6 Flatten the top of the paper into a square shape. You now have a square base.

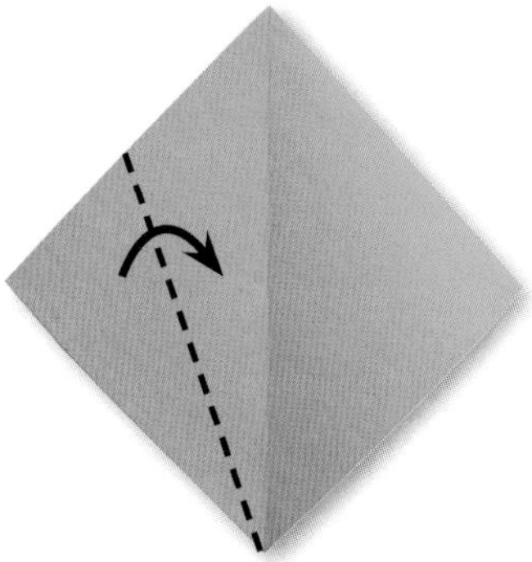

1 Start with a square base (see page 7), with the open end facing you. Fold the left-hand point of the top layer to the central crease.

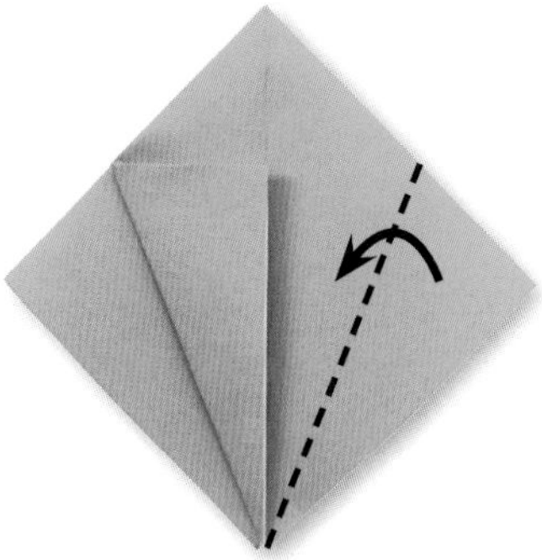

2 Do the same on the other side.

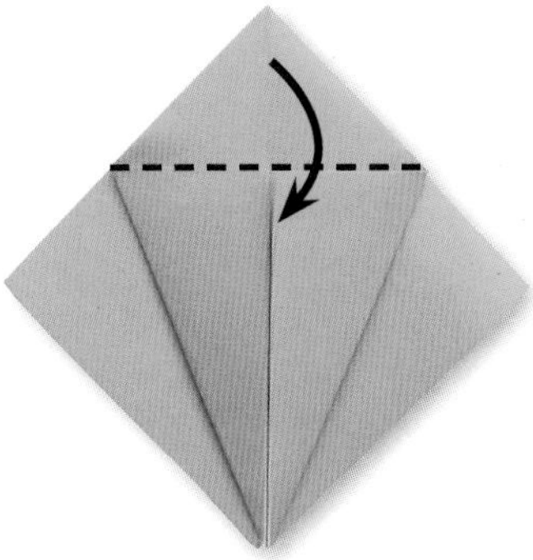

3 Valley fold the top point down.

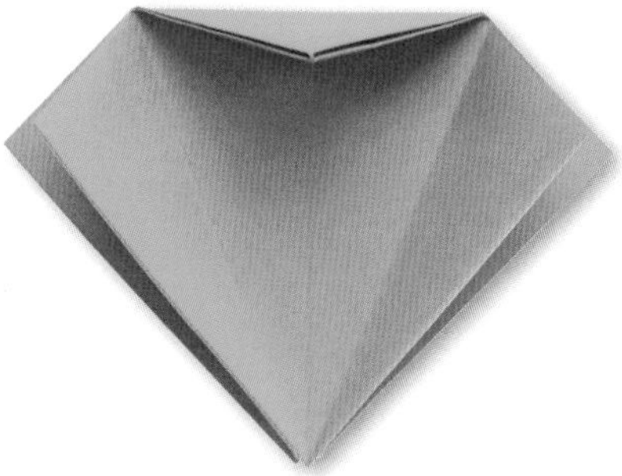

4 Unfold the top and sides and you have the shape shown here.

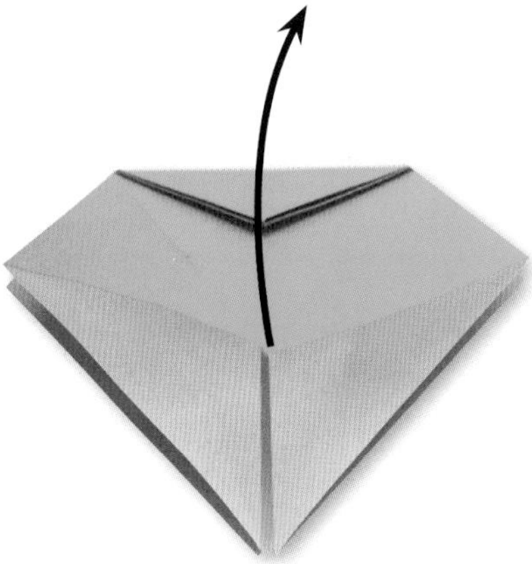

5 Take the bottom corner and lift it up to the top.

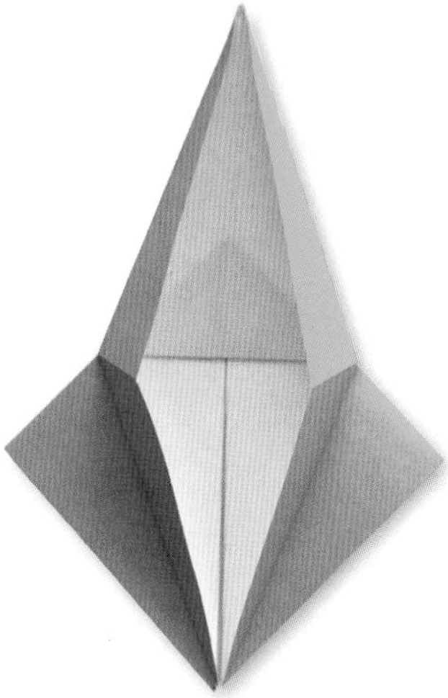

6 The paper should open like a bird's beak. Open out the flap as far as it will go.

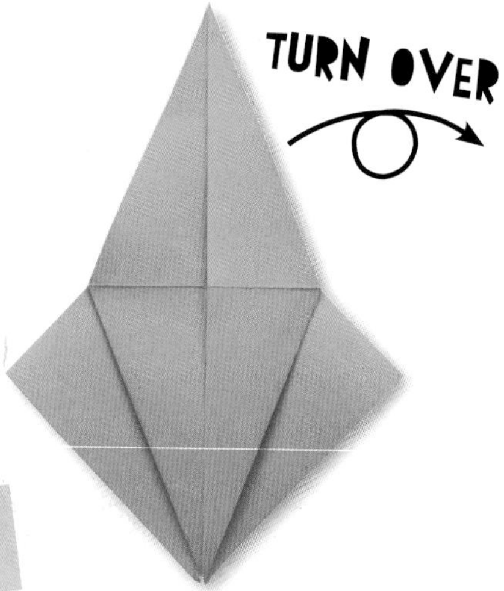

TURN OVER

7 Flatten the paper down so that you now have this shape. Turn the paper over.

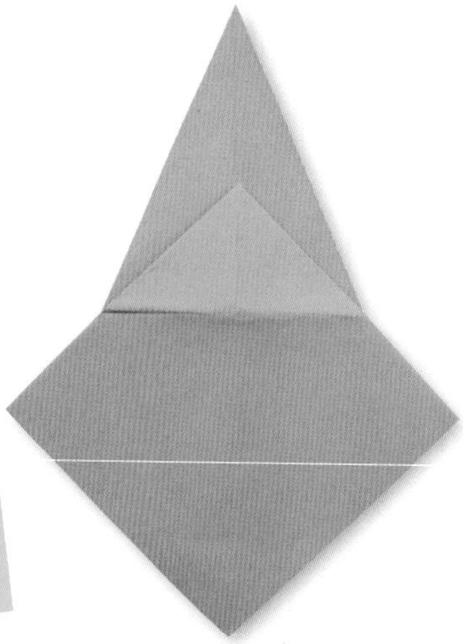

8 The paper should now look like this. Repeat steps 1 to 7 on this side as well.

9 You now have a bird base. The two flaps at the bottom should be separated by an open slit.

DINO FUN

Let's begin exploring the world of dinosaur origami with some fun projects. In this chapter, you'll learn how to make everything from a dinosaur egg and sharp dino claws to a blinking eye and a snapping raptor head.

JURASSIC EYE

Follow the steps to find out what it's like to stare a dinosaur right in the eye. Let's see who blinks first!

1
Place your paper like this, white side up, with a corner facing you. Fold in half from right to left, then unfold.

2
Now fold it in half from top to bottom and unfold.

3
Fold the top point down to the central crease.

4
Fold the bottom point up to the central crease.

5
Fold the top edge down to the central crease.

6
Fold the bottom edge up to the central crease.

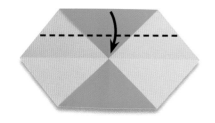

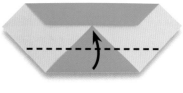

7 Your paper should look like. Unfold all the folds you made in steps 3 to 6.

UNFOLD ↑

UNFOLD ↓

8 Fold the top point down to the second crease.

9 Repeat step 8 with the bottom point.

10 Fold the top edge down to the third crease.

11 Repeat step 10 with the bottom edge.

12 Fold the top edge down to the central crease.

TURN OVER

13 Fold the bottom edge up to the central crease.

14 Your paper should look like this. Turn it over from left to right.

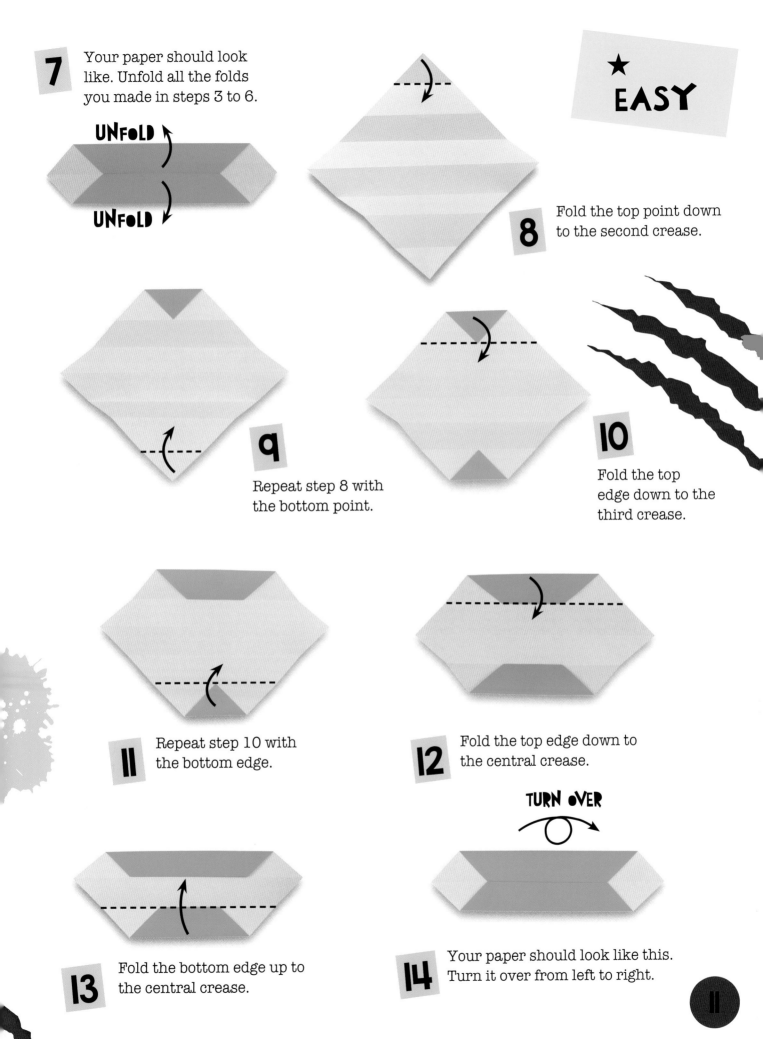

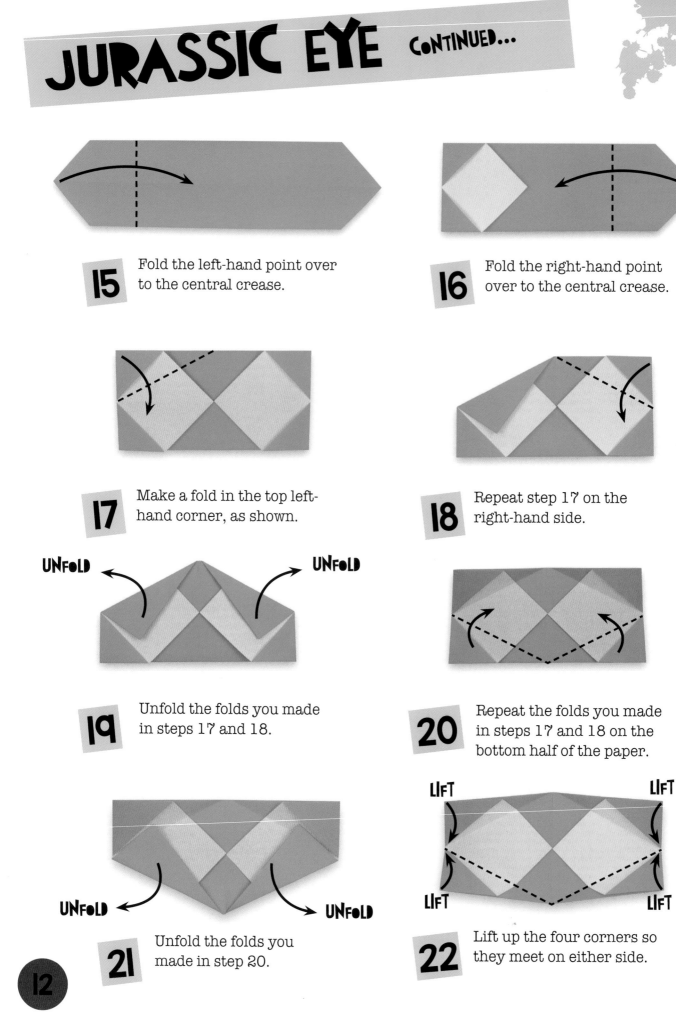

15 Fold the left-hand point over to the central crease.

16 Fold the right-hand point over to the central crease.

17 Make a fold in the top left-hand corner, as shown.

18 Repeat step 17 on the right-hand side.

UNFOLD   UNFOLD

19 Unfold the folds you made in steps 17 and 18.

20 Repeat the folds you made in steps 17 and 18 on the bottom half of the paper.

UNFOLD   UNFOLD

21 Unfold the folds you made in step 20.

LIFT   LIFT
LIFT   LIFT

22 Lift up the four corners so they meet on either side.

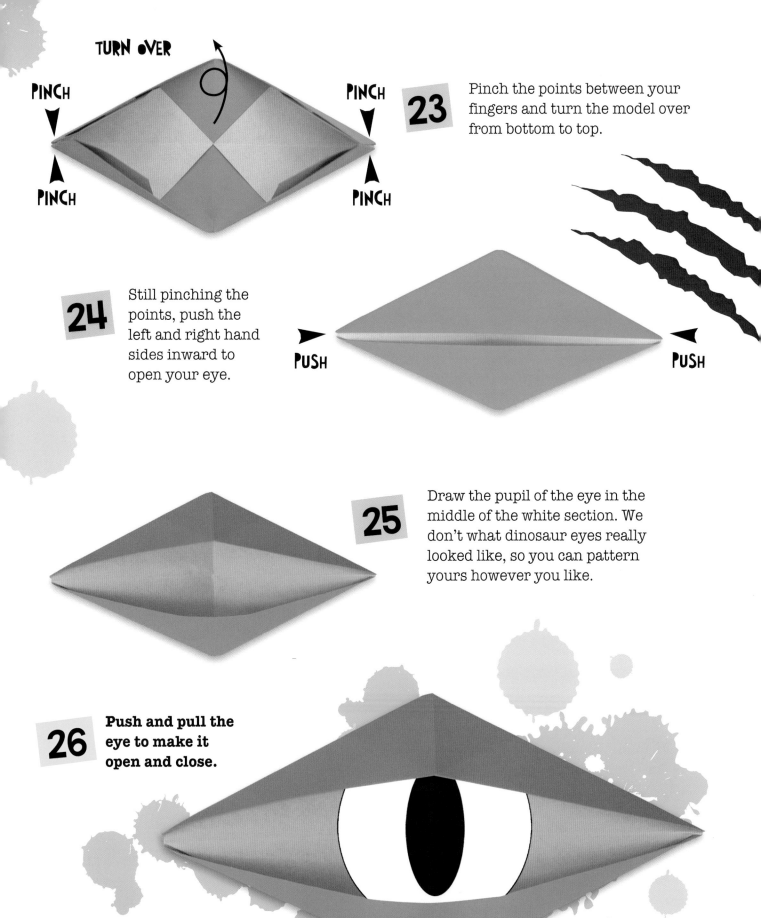

TURN OVER

PINCH

PINCH

PINCH

PINCH

23 Pinch the points between your fingers and turn the model over from bottom to top.

24 Still pinching the points, push the left and right hand sides inward to open your eye.

PUSH

PUSH

25 Draw the pupil of the eye in the middle of the white section. We don't what dinosaur eyes really looked like, so you can pattern yours however you like.

26 Push and pull the eye to make it open and close.

FINISHED!

DINOSAUR EGG

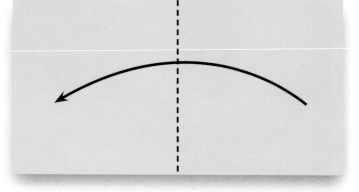

All dinosaurs started life as an egg. Why not make several eggs so you can have your very own dinosaur nest?

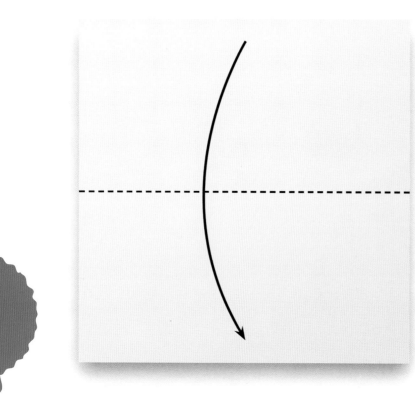

1

Place your paper like this, white side up, with a straight edge facing you. Fold in half from top to bottom.

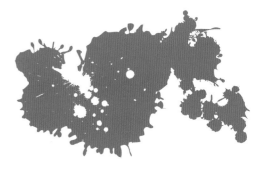

2

Fold the paper in half from right to left.

UNFOLD

3 Unfold the fold you made in step 2.

4 Fold the top right-hand corner over to the central crease.

TURN OVER

5 Turn the paper over from left to right and repeat step 4 on that side. Then turn the paper back over again.

OPEN ↑

6 Your paper should look like this. Open the folds out at the bottom a little.

LIFT

7 Holding the upper two layers at the bottom, lift them up and over to the top left. The paper should form a square shape.

8 Your paper should look like this. Rotate it to the left slightly so the open pointed flaps are facing you.

45°

9

Valley fold both layers of
the right-hand point over as
shown. The fold should be
slightly slanted.

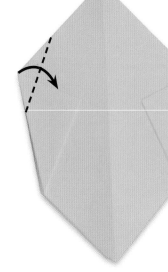

10

Repeat step 9 on
the left-hand side.

11

Mountain fold the
upper flap on both
sides back behind
the paper.

12

Make a small
valley fold in
the upper layer
on the left-hand
side, as shown.

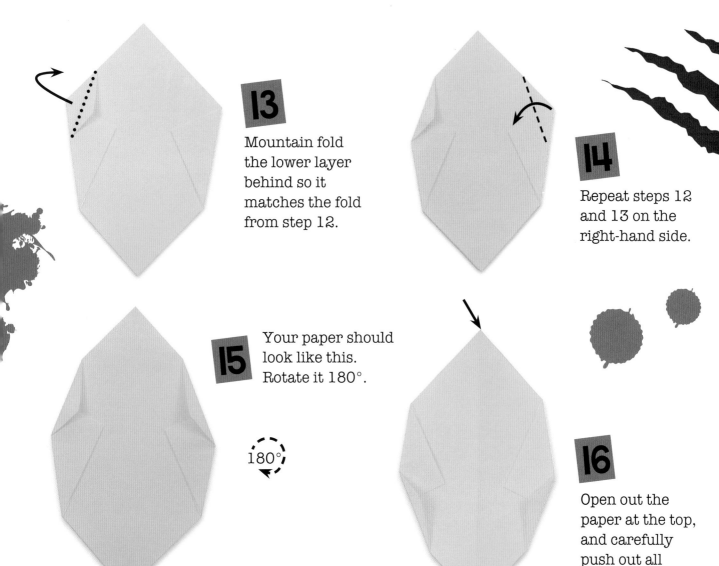

13 Mountain fold the lower layer behind so it matches the fold from step 12.

14 Repeat steps 12 and 13 on the right-hand side.

15 Your paper should look like this. Rotate it 180°.

180°

16 Open out the paper at the top, and carefully push out all four sides.

17 And there's your egg, but where's the baby dino? It looks like it's already hatched and has scuttled away. Don't worry, you can catch up with him on the next page.

FINISHED!

17

BABY DINOSAUR

Now you've made the eggs, it's time to fold a baby dinosaur or two. This is quite a simple project, but you'll need to make sure you crease your folds well.

1

Let's start by making a kite base. Place your paper like this, white side up with a corner facing you. Fold it in half from right to left.

2

Unfold the fold you made in step 1.

UNFOLD

3

Fold the left-hand point over to the central crease.

4

Fold the right-hand point over to the central crease.

5

Now you've got a kite base, fold the left-hand point over to the central crease.

6

Fold the right-hand point over to the central crease.

7

Fold the paper in half from bottom to top.

8

Fold the top points (both layers) down, as shown.

q

Fold the bottom point of the top layer back up.

10 Fold the paper in half from left to right.

11 Your paper should look like this. Rotate it to the right so it matches the image in step 12.

90°

12 Valley fold the top left-hand point over, as shown.

13 Fold it the other way so it's also a mountain fold, then turn it into an inside reverse fold (see page 5). This is the head.

14 Fold the tip of the head over.

20

15 Fold it the other way, so it's also a mountain fold, then fold it up inside the head to form an inside reverse fold.

FLATTEN

16 Your paper should look like this. Flatten it down.

17 Carefully pull the legs apart.

PULL

PULL

18 Your baby dinosaur should be able to stand up, although he might be a bit unsteady on his feet at first.

FINISHED!

DINO CLAWS

If you've ever wondered what it would be like to be a dinosaur, then this is the project for you. You'll need ten pieces of paper to make the full set of claws.

180°

START WITH A KITE BASE

1

Let's start with the first claw. Begin by making a kite base (see page 6), then rotate the paper 180°.

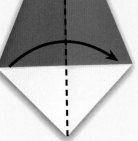

2

Fold the paper in half from left to right.

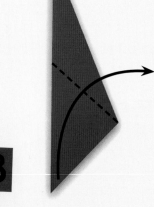

3

Fold the bottom point up and to the right.

TURN OVER

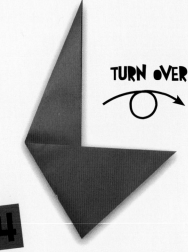

4

Turn your paper over from right to left.

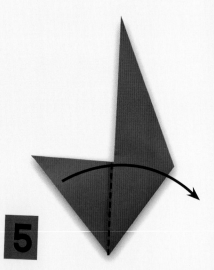

5

Fold the left-hand point over to the right.

6 Turn the paper over again from right to left

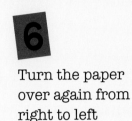

7 Fold the left-hand point up and to the right along the fold line you made in step 3.

8 Now mountain fold the point over, tucking it behind the second layer of paper.

q Open the paper up at the top on the right-hand side.

90°

10 Your paper should look like this. Rotate it 90° to the right.

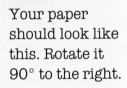

INSERT FINGER

11 To put on your first claw, insert your finger into the opening you made in step 9 and push it into the paper.

 12 Repeat all the steps nine more times and you'll have a full set of claws.

FINISHED!

23

DINOSAUR FOOTPRINTS

We don't know about dinosaurs just through their fossilized bones but also through preserved footprints. Here's how to make a couple of giant dino steps.

1

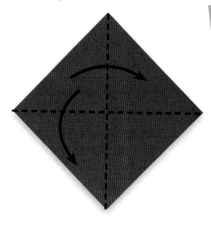

Position your paper like this, white side down, with a corner facing you. Fold it in half from left to right, and unfold. Then fold it in half from top to bottom, and unfold.

2

Use your scissors to cut the paper in half along one of the crease lines, as shown.

3

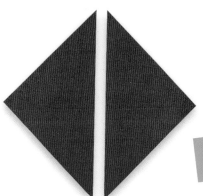

Put the right-hand piece of paper to one side.

4

Turn the remaining piece of paper over from top to bottom.

TURN OVER

5

Fold the bottom point up and to the right so that the lower left edge lines up with the central crease.

6

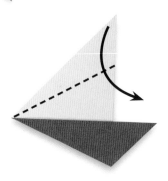

Repeat step 5 on the top point.

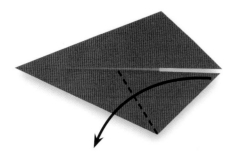

7 Lift the bottom-right point up and then down to the left.

8 Before you flatten the fold down, make a new fold on the bottom right-hand side, as shown, then flatten both folds down.

9 Your paper should look like this. Repeat steps 7 and 8 at the top.

10 Get your other piece of paper and repeat steps 4 to 9.

FINISHED!

TURN OVER

11 Turn your pieces of paper over from top to bottom.

12 Position your models a step apart so they look like real footprints. Why not make some more for a dino that went on a long walk?

SNAPPING RAPTOR

Follow the instructions to make the snapping head of a fierce type of dino known as a raptor—there are other raptors to make on pages 30 and 46.

START WITH A KITE BASE

180°

1
Begin by making a kite base (see page 6), then rotate the paper 180°.

2
Fold the right-hand point over to the central crease.

3
Repeat step 2 on the other side.

4
Fold the paper in half from bottom to top.

5
Fold the top point of the upper layer down to the bottom edge.

6
Fold the top point of the lower layer over and to the right.

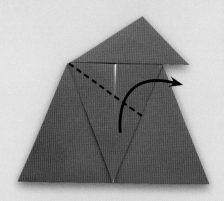

7 Fold the bottom point up and to the right.

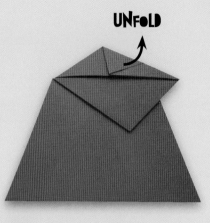

UNFOLD

8 Fold the top point down to where the flaps meet, using the crease you made earlier as a guide.

9 Unfold the fold you made in step 8.

UNFOLD

10 Now unfold the fold you made in step 6.

TUCK

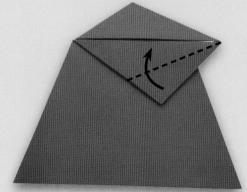

11 Make an inside reverse fold (see page 5) by tucking the right edge inside.

FLATTEN

12 Your paper should look like this. Flatten it down.

13 Make a small fold, as shown.

14 Unfold the fold you made in step 13.

UNFOLD

15 Now unfold the fold you made in step 7.

UNFOLD

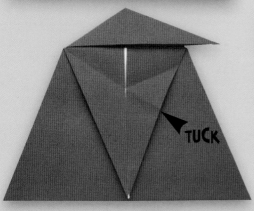

TUCK

16 Repeat step 11 on this side too, making an inside reverse fold by tucking the right edge inside.

FLATTEN

17 Flatten the paper down. This is your raptor's head.

18 Mountain fold the lower half of the paper in half to create the neck.

19 Add some eyes and teeth to give your dino a fierce expression. If you open and close the neck, the raptor will snap its jaws.

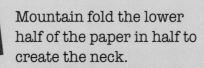

OPEN AND CLOSE

OPEN AND CLOSE

FINISHED!

MEAT EATERS

Let's journey back in time to when the world was ruled by (paper) monsters. This chapter will show you how to make the deadliest dinos of all—the meat eaters!

VeloCiraptor

Say "veh-LOSS-ih-RAP-tor"

Though small and covered in feathers, Velociraptor was still a deadly predator—like a sort of savage turkey. They probably hunted in packs, so why not make a whole group of them?

START WITH A BIRD BASE

1 Start by making a bird base (see page 8). Then valley fold the top point of the upper layer down to the bottom.

2 Valley fold the paper in half from right to left. Then rotate the paper 90° to the left so a corner is facing you and the open flaps are on the right.

FOLD BACK

3 Take the left hand point and peel up and to the right so it reveals the small triangle of paper shown in step 4.

4 Flatten the paper down.

FLATTEN

5 Valley fold the top point over to the left, as shown.

6

Fold it the other way so it's also a mountain fold, then turn it into an outside reverse fold (see page 5). This is the head.

7

Tuck the tip of the nose inside the head by making an inside reverse fold (see page 5).

8

Valley fold the left-hand point down, as shown.

q

Fold it the other way so it's also a mountain fold, then turn it into an inside reverse fold to make the hands.

10

Fold the right-hand point of the upper layer down and to the left to form the first leg.

11

Valley fold the bottom point over to the left to form the first foot.

12

Your paper should look like this. Repeat steps 10 and 11 on the other side.

13

Finally, use your pens to give Velociraptor a feathery coat.

MEGALOSAURUS

Say "MEG-ah-low-SAW-rus"

In 1824, this was the first dinosaur to be given a proper scientific name, which means "giant lizard." Of course, it wasn't a lizard at all, but a great two-legged hunter that roamed the Earth around 166 million years ago.

START WITH A BIRD BASE

1 Start by making a bird base (see page 8). Then, fold the left-hand point of the upper layer over to the right.

2 Your paper should look like this. Turn it over from left to right.

TURN OVER

3 Fold the left-hand point of the upper layer over to the right on this side too.

4 Your paper should now look like this with a clear gap between the top two points. Rotate it 90° to the right.

90°

5 Valley fold the left-hand point of the upper layer all the way over to the right.

6 Valley fold the paper in half from bottom to top, as shown.

7 Valley fold the left-hand point up.

8 Fold it the other way so it's also a mountain fold, then turn it into an inside reverse fold (see page 5).

9 Valley fold the left-hand point down, as shown.

10 Mountain fold it the other way, then unfold.

11 Make another diagonal valley fold just below the fold you made in steps 9 and 10. Fold it the other way, so it's also a mountain fold, then unfold.

PUSH ▶

12 Push the top left point down and to the right so that folds go out on either side of the paper, forming a step fold. Flatten the paper down. This is the head.

MEGALOSAURUS CONTINUED...

13

Fold the right-hand point of the upper layer down and to the left to form the first leg.

14

TURN OVER

Your paper should look like this. Turn it over from left to right and repeat step 13 on the other side

15

TURN OVER

Turn the paper back over again from right to left.

16

Fold the bottom point of the upper layer up and to the right to form the first foot.

17

Your paper should look like this. Repeat step 16 on the other side to form the other foot.

18

Using scissors, make a small cut right through the paper, as shown.

19

Valley fold the upper layer of paper to the left of your cut to make the first arm.

20

Your paper should look like this. Repeat step 19 on the other side.

21

Make a valley fold in the top left-hand point, then fold it the other way so it's also a mountain fold.

TUCK ▶

22

Push the left-hand point down and to the right to form an inside reverse fold. Tuck it inside to form the snout.

23

Draw in your dinosaur's features— be sure to give it sharp teeth! Now your Megalosaurus is ready to go on its first hunt.

FINISHED!

T. REX

Say "tie-RAN-oh-SAW-rus REX"

As long as a bus, with keen eyesight and a mouth full of razor-sharp teeth, Tyrannosaurus rex was one of the fiercest creatures ever to walk the Earth.

START WITH A BIRD BASE

SWING BACK

1

Make a bird base (see page 8). Then fold the left point of the upper layer over to the right.

2

Take the right flap at the very back of the paper and swing it to the left, so that two points are revealed at the top, as shown in step 3.

3

Fold the bottom point of the upper layer up to the top.

4

Valley fold the bottom corner of the upper right flap into the middle.

5

Do the same on the other side.

6

The paper should now look like this. Turn the paper over from left to right.

TURN OVER

PULL

7

Gently pull out the tall point on the right into the position shown in step 8.

PULL

8

Do the same on the other side. Then mountain fold the tip of the central triangle.

9

Valley fold the bottom section over to the right as shown here.

10

The paper should now look like this.

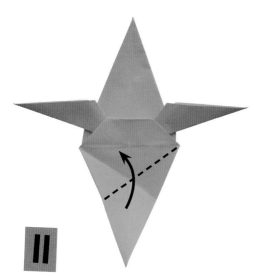
11

Unfold, then valley fold the bottom section over to the left.

CREASE MARKS

12

Unfold and you should have the crease marks as shown here.

37

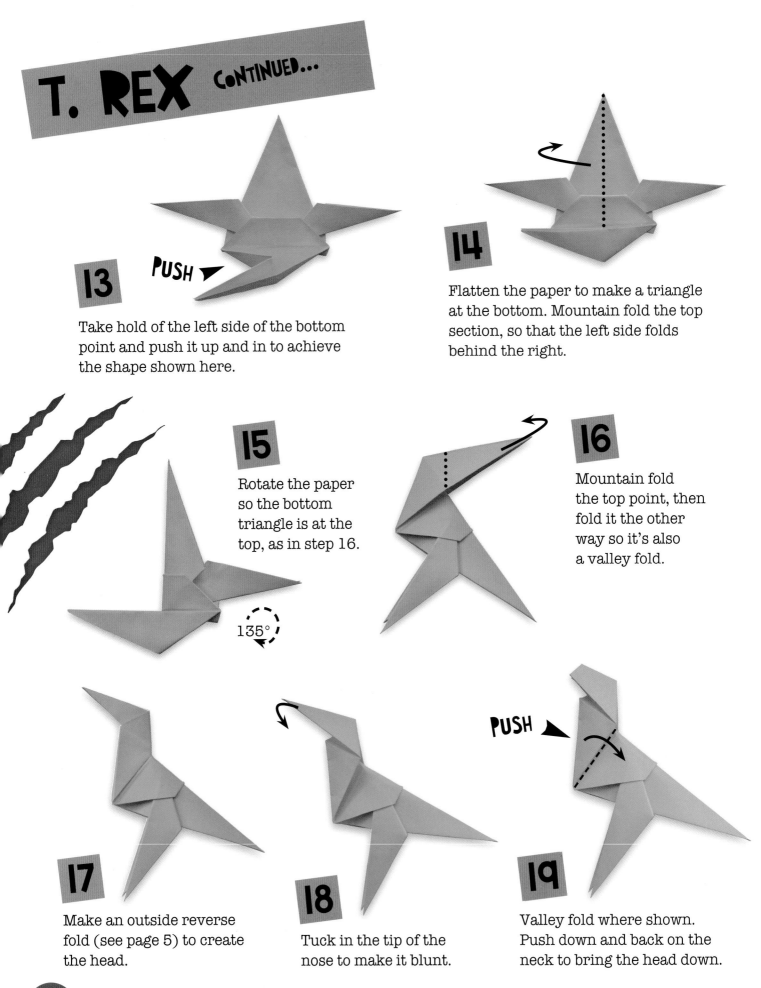

13

PUSH ▶

Take hold of the left side of the bottom point and push it up and in to achieve the shape shown here.

14

Flatten the paper to make a triangle at the bottom. Mountain fold the top section, so that the left side folds behind the right.

15

Rotate the paper so the bottom triangle is at the top, as in step 16.

135°

16

Mountain fold the top point, then fold it the other way so it's also a valley fold.

17

Make an outside reverse fold (see page 5) to create the head.

18

Tuck in the tip of the nose to make it blunt.

19

PUSH ▶

Valley fold where shown. Push down and back on the neck to bring the head down.

20 Valley fold the bottom section over to the right as shown.

21 Fold it the other way, so it's also a mountain fold, then make an inside reverse fold (see page 5).

22 Flatten the paper down.

FLATTEN

23 Pull the toe tip forward and make another inside reverse fold to create the foot.

24 Repeat steps 20 to 23 on the other side.

25 Push the head down a bit more to make it look big and scary. You have created the king of the dinosaurs!

FINISHED!

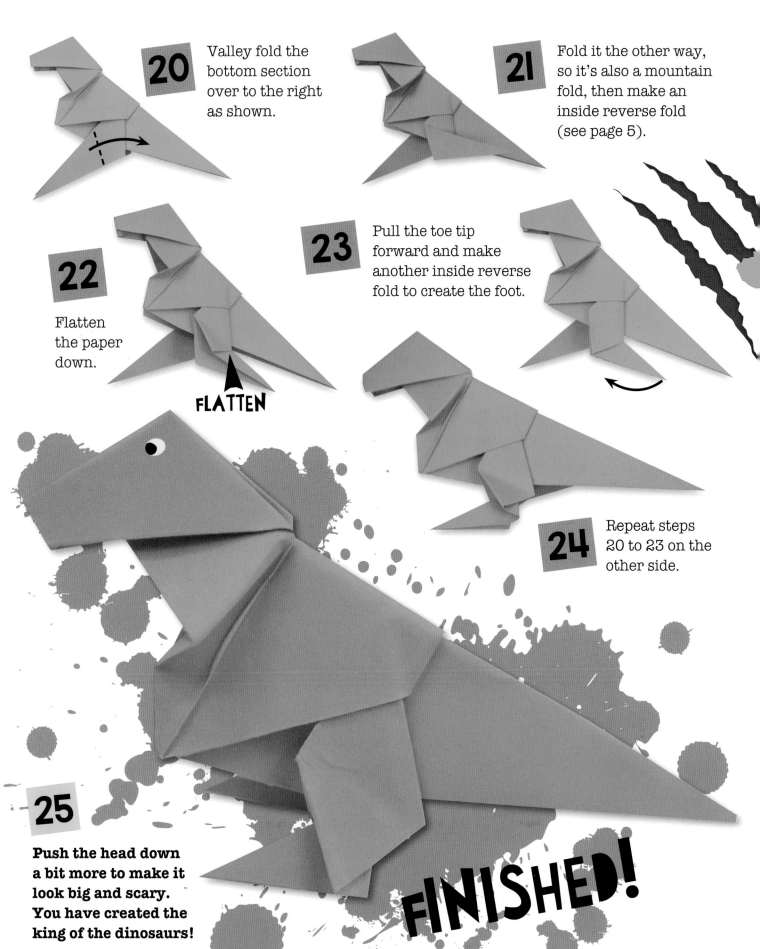

SPINOSAURUS

Say "SPY-noh-SAW-rus"

This fierce predator had a large sail on its back and probably spent most of its time in water, hunting for fish and other marine creatures.

START WITH A BIRD BASE

1 Start by making a bird base (see page 8). Then valley fold the top point of the upper layer down to the bottom.

2 Mountain fold the remaining top point down to the bottom.

3 Your paper should look like this. Fold the top point down to the horizontal crease, and then unfold.

4 Fold the top point down to the crease you made in step 3.

5 Your paper should look like this. Unfold the last fold.

6

Turn the paper over from left to right and repeat steps 4 and 5 on the other side.

7

Fold the right-hand point of the upper layer over to the left, and repeat steps 4 and 5. Then fold the point back to the right again.

8

Now, fold the left-hand point of the upper layer over to the right, and repeat steps 4 and 5 on that side too. Then fold the point back to the left again.

9

Open out the folds at the bottom.

OPEN   OPEN

PUSH

10

Start pushing down the top point.

PUSH

11

As you push, the creases made in steps 4 to 8 should start folding in on themselves.

PUSH   PUSH

12

Start pushing the sides back together. When the top point is completely inside the rest of the paper, flatten down the paper.

SPINOSAURUS CONTINUED...

13

Fold the bottom point of the upper layer up and to the right, as shown.

14

Unfold.

UNFOLD

15

Fold the bottom point of the upper layer up and to the left.

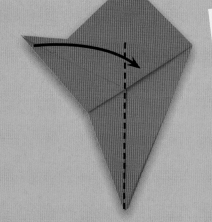

16

Start to fold the top left-hand point over to the right along the central crease, but only fold it halfway.

PUSH

17

As you fold the left point across the halfway point, start pushing the paper up so it forms a pocket.

TURN OVER

FLATTEN

18

Flatten the paper down, then turn it over from right to left.

19

Fold the bottom point of the upper layer up and to the left, then unfold.

20

Now fold the bottom point up and to the right.

21

Repeat step 16 on the opposite side by folding the top right-hand point over to the left along the central crease. Only fold it halfway.

22

PUSH

As you fold the point across the halfway point, start pushing the paper up so it forms a pocket, then flatten it down.

TURN OVER

PULL

23

Your paper should look like this. Turn it over from left to right.

24

Take the bottom left-hand point and pull it out to the left and up, so it forms an inside reverse fold (see page 5).

PULL

25

Keep pulling the paper up until it's level with the fold you made in step 22, then flatten it down.

26

Your paper should look like this. Repeat steps 24 and 25 on the other side.

27

Make a valley fold, as shown, folding the point second from the right over to the left.

28

Tuck the bottom point behind by making a small mountain fold. Repeat on the other side.

SPINOSAURUS CONTINUED...

TURN OVER

29 Take the point you folded across in step 27 and fold it down and to the right.

30 Turn your paper over from left to right and repeat steps 27 and 29 on the other side. Then turn the paper back again.

31 Make a mountain fold on the upper layer of the right-hand side, as shown. Repeat on the lower layer.

32 Your paper should look like this. Repeat step 31 on the left-hand side.

TURN OVER

33 Fold the bottom point over to the left to form the first foot.

34 Turn the paper over from left to right and repeat step 33 on the other side to form the other foot.

35 Mountain fold the upper layer on the right-hand side, as shown. Repeat on the lower layer. This is the tail.

36 Valley fold the left-hand point up and to the right.

37

Now fold the point down and to the left.

38

Pull the point to the left, then push it back to the right so that folds go out on either side of the paper, forming a step fold. This is the head.

PUSH ▶

FOLDS GO EITHER SIDE OF PAPER

39

Push the tip of the left-hand point down and to the right.

PUSH ◀

40

Tuck the point inside the head to form the snout.

PUSH ◀

41

Your paper should look like this. All that's left now is to stand your Spinosaurus on its feet.

42

Give your dino big eyes to help it track down its prey.

FINISHED!

UTAHRAPTOR

Say "YOO-tah-RAP-tor"

This dinosaur was a fast, agile predator that roamed the USA around 125 million years ago. It had one enormous claw on each of its hind legs.

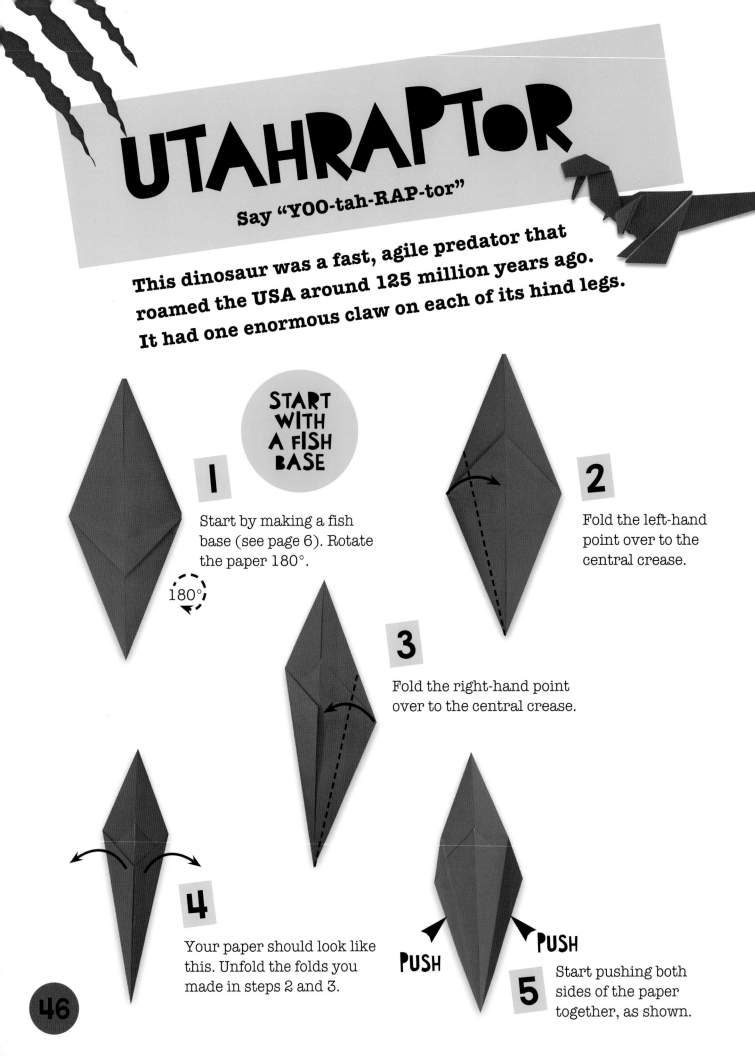

START WITH A FISH BASE

1 Start by making a fish base (see page 6). Rotate the paper 180°.

180°

2 Fold the left-hand point over to the central crease.

3 Fold the right-hand point over to the central crease.

4 Your paper should look like this. Unfold the folds you made in steps 2 and 3.

5 Start pushing both sides of the paper together, as shown.

PUSH   PUSH

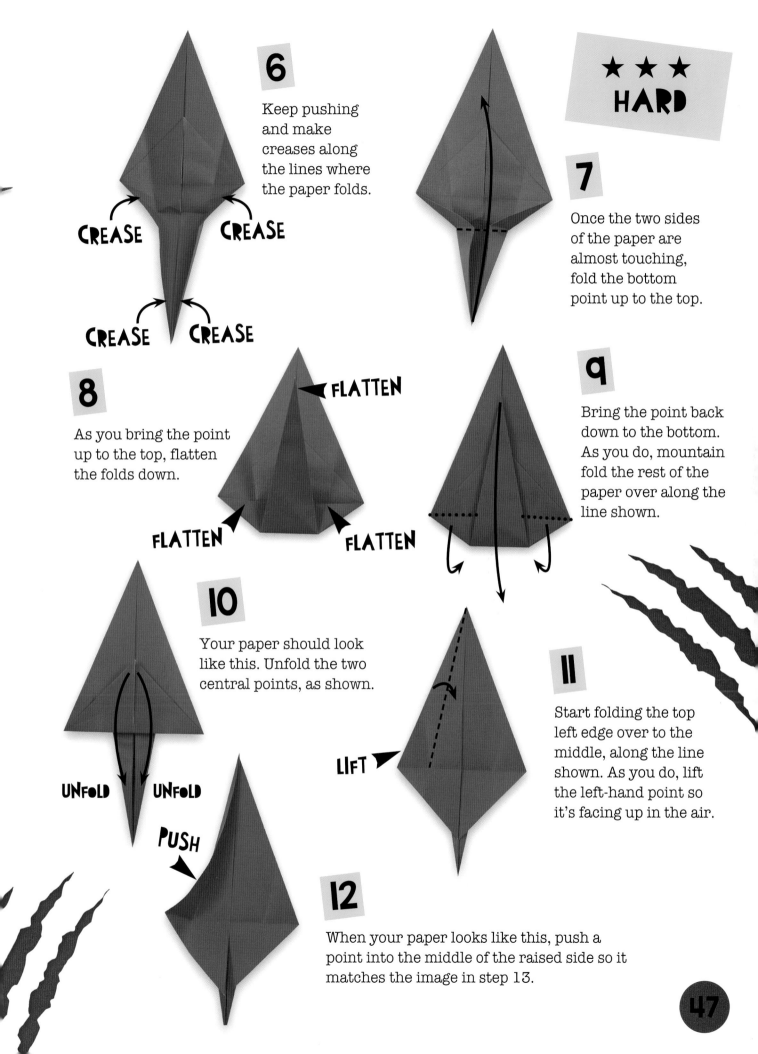

6

Keep pushing and make creases along the lines where the paper folds.

CREASE CREASE

CREASE CREASE

★ ★ ★
HARD

7

Once the two sides of the paper are almost touching, fold the bottom point up to the top.

8

As you bring the point up to the top, flatten the folds down.

◀ FLATTEN

FLATTEN ▶   ◀ FLATTEN

q

Bring the point back down to the bottom. As you do, mountain fold the rest of the paper over along the line shown.

10

Your paper should look like this. Unfold the two central points, as shown.

UNFOLD   UNFOLD

PUSH
◀

11

Start folding the top left edge over to the middle, along the line shown. As you do, lift the left-hand point so it's facing up in the air.

LIFT ▶

12

When your paper looks like this, push a point into the middle of the raised side so it matches the image in step 13.

47

13

Fold the point you made in step 12 over to the middle. As you do, bring the left-hand point up and over to the middle and the bottom left-hand point over to the right-hand side. Flatten the paper down.

14

Valley fold the right-hand point of the upper layer back over to the left.

15

Repeat step 11 on the other side

16

Repeat steps 12 and 13 on the other side. Remember to bring the right-hand point over to the middle and the bottom right-hand point over to the left so it matches up with the left-hand point.

17

Valley fold the left-hand point of the upper layer back to the right.

18

Mountain fold the paper in half from right to left.

19

Your paper should look like this. Rotate it 90° to the left.

90°

20

Valley fold the bottom point of the upper layer over to the left.

21

Repeat step 20 on the other side.

22

Your paper should look like this. Valley fold the left-hand point up and to the right.

23

Fold it the other way, so it's also a mountain fold, then turn it into an outside reverse fold (see page 5).

24

Your paper should look like this. Valley fold the top point down and over to the left.

25

Fold it the other way, so it's also a mountain fold, then turn it into an outside reverse fold. This is the head.

26

Open up the head up so it's flat. Then mountain fold the end down, as shown.

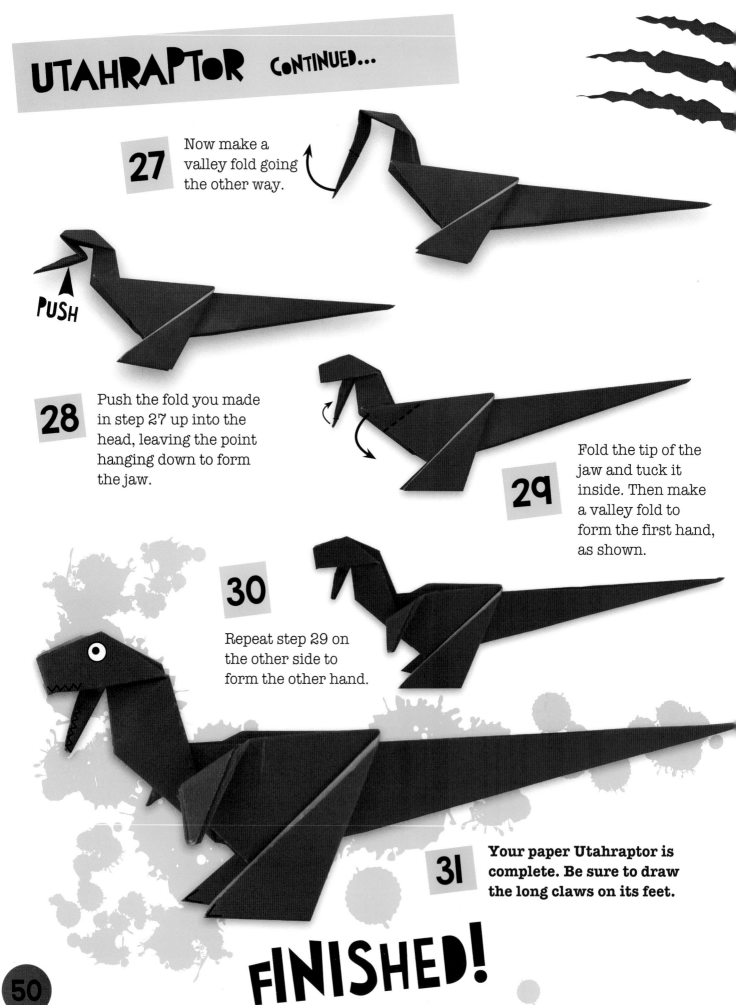

27 Now make a valley fold going the other way.

PUSH

28 Push the fold you made in step 27 up into the head, leaving the point hanging down to form the jaw.

29 Fold the tip of the jaw and tuck it inside. Then make a valley fold to form the first hand, as shown.

30 Repeat step 29 on the other side to form the other hand.

31 Your paper Utahraptor is complete. Be sure to draw the long claws on its feet.

FINISHED!

PLANT EATERS

Here are seven plant-eating dinosaurs for you to fold. Some have long necks, some have horns and crests, while others have spiky back plates.

IGUANODON

Say "ig-WAH-noh-don"

The Iguanodon had giant spiky thumbs which it could use to fight off predators. This origami dino will require two pieces of paper: one for the body and one for the legs.

BODY

START WITH A KITE BASE

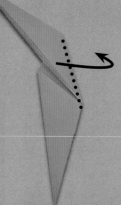

1 Take your first piece of paper and make a kite base (see page 6). Then rotate your paper 180°.

180°

2 Fold the bottom left and right-hand corners in to meet the central crease.

3 Mountain fold the paper in half along the central crease, from right to left.

4 Valley fold the top point over to the left, as shown.

5 Crease well and then fold back to the right, so it's also a mountain fold. Then turn it into an inside reverse fold (see page 5).

6

Your paper should
look like this. Valley
fold the top point
back on itself, as
shown. Crease well.

UNFOLD

7

Unfold the crease
you made in step 6.

UNFOLD

8

Valley fold the top tip
back again—this time
folding it to the right.

q

Unfold the
fold you
made in
step 8.

PUSH

10

Now push the central crease
down over the two folds you
made in steps 6 to 8 to create
a step fold (see page 4). This is
the head.

11

Your paper should now
look like this. Fold the
end of the head over,
as shown.

 TUCK

12

Tuck the fold
into the head.

13

Your Iguanodon's
body is ready.
Put it to one side
while you make
the legs.

LEGS

START
WITH A
WATERBOMB
BASE

↻ 90°

1 Take the other piece of paper and make a waterbomb base (see page 7). Rotate it 90° to the left, so the tip of the triangle is facing left.

2 Valley fold the left-hand point to the right-hand edge of the paper.

3 Unfold the fold you made in step 2.

UNFOLD

4 Take hold of the upper layer of paper on the right-hand side and lift it over to the left, creating two pocket shapes.

LIFT

FLATTEN

FLATTEN

5 Your paper should look like this. Flatten it down at the top and bottom to create two white triangle shapes.

6

Fold the left-hand side (including the green triangle at the back) to the middle line, so the left-hand edge meets the central crease.

7

Make four valley folds, as shown. These are the feet. Now rotate your paper 180°.

180°

8

Dab some glue in the shaded areas. Then fetch the iguanodon body.

q

Place the body in the middle of the legs. Fold the legs down over the body.

10

Press the paper down hard, so that the legs stick to the body. Phew! After all that folding, your Iguanodon is ready to munch some leaves for lunch!

BRACHIOSAURUS

Say "BRACK-ee-oh-SAW-rus"

A bit like an enormous giraffe, this dino was one of the tallest creatures that has ever lived. You'll need a pair of scissors to complete this project.

START WITH A KITE BASE

1 Start by making a kite base (see page 6), then fold the paper in half from left to right.

2 Rotate the paper to the right so that it matches the image in step 3.

3 Fold the top point over to the right, as shown.

4 Fold it the other way, so it's also a mountain fold, then turn it into an outside reverse fold (see page 5).

FLATTEN

5 Your paper should look like this. Flatten it down.

6 Fold the top point over to the left, as shown.

7 Fold it the other way, so it's also a mountain fold, then turn this into an outside reverse fold too.

FLATTEN

8 Your paper should look like this. Flatten it down. This is the head.

TUCK ▶

9 Fold the top point over.

10 Tuck the point into the head to form the nose.

11 Fold the bottom right point over to the left, as shown. Then fold it the other way, so it's also a mountain fold.

12 Make a smaller fold back to the right. Again fold it the other way, so it's also a mountain fold.

13 Now turn the folds you made in steps 11 and 12 into two inside reverse folds (see page 5), one inside the other. This is the tail.

14 Flatten the paper down.

FLATTEN

15 Use scissors to cut a rectangle from the bottom to make the legs.

16 And that's your dino complete. It can now use its long neck to eat leaves right at the tops of trees.

57

PARASAUROLOPHUS

Say "PAR-uh-SAW-roh-LOW-fuss"

This dino had a long crest on top of its head, which it may have used to call to other dinos— a bit like a trumpet. Again, you'll need two pieces of paper to make this distinctive looking creature.

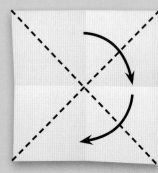

LEGS

I

Let's start with the legs this time. Place your paper white side up with a straight edge facing you. Valley fold in half from top to bottom, and unfold. Then valley fold in half from left to right, and unfold.

2

Diagonally fold the top-left corner to the bottom right, and unfold. Then diagonally fold the top right corner down to the bottom left, and unfold.

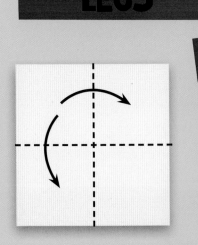

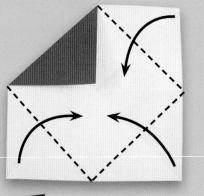

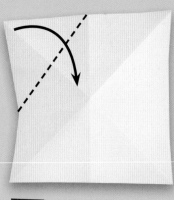

UNFOLD UNFOLD UNFOLD UNFOLD

3

Fold the top left corner over to the central point.

4

Repeat step 3 on the other three corners.

5

Unfold the folds you made in steps 3 and 4.

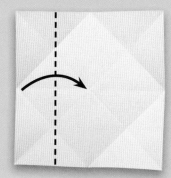

6 Fold the left edge over to the middle.

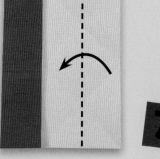

7 Repeat step 6 on the other side.

8 Fold the top edge down to the middle.

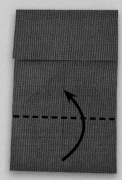

9 Fold the bottom edge up to the middle.

UNFOLD

10 Unfold the fold you made in step 10 about halfway.

11 Pull the central point of the second layer down and to the left so it forms a triangle shape, as in the image for step 12.

12 Repeat step 11 on the right-hand side

FLATTEN

13 Flatten the paper down.

14 Your paper should look like this. Repeat steps 10 to 13 on the bottom half.

15 Fold the top left-hand point up and to the right, as shown.

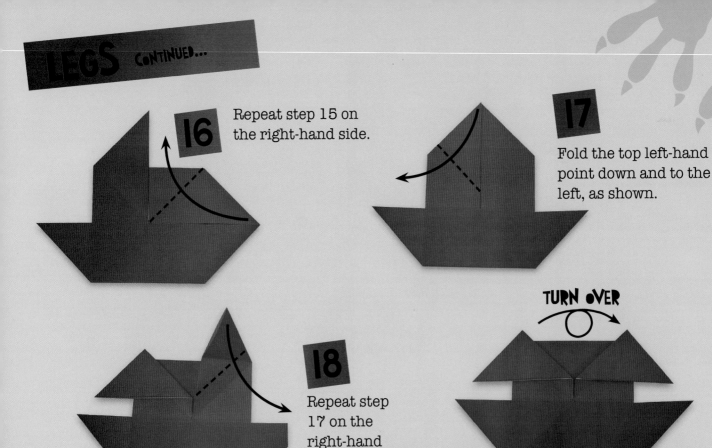

16 Repeat step 15 on the right-hand side.

17 Fold the top left-hand point down and to the left, as shown.

18 Repeat step 17 on the right-hand side.

TURN OVER

19 Your paper should look like this. Turn it over from left to right.

20 Fold over the top of the paper so that two small triangles are showing.

21 Fold the bottom edge up so it's level with the bottom two points.

22 Fold the bottom left- and bottom right-hand points so they're sticking straight up toward you.

23 These are your Parasaurolophus legs. Put them to one side while you get on with the body.

1 Take your other piece of paper and place it like this, white side up with a corner facing you. Valley fold it in half from right to left and unfold.

2 Fold the bottom right edge up to the top-left edge.

3 Unfold the fold you made in step 2.

UNFOLD

4 Fold the right-hand point so it touches the crease you made in step 2.

5 Fold the left-hand point across so the edges line up, as in the image in step 6.

6 Fold the top left edge over to the central crease. The new crease should go where the edges line up.

7 Fold the bottom left-hand point over to the central crease.

8 Repeat step 7 on the right-hand side.

9

Your paper should look like this. Fold it in half from left to right.

10

Now take your dinosaur's legs. Place the body over the legs. Make sure it lines up as in the image in step 11.

11

Fold the top point of the body down and to the right, making sure it lines up with the legs.

12

Now fold the point up and to the left.

13

Your two pieces of paper should look like this. Put the dinosaur's legs to one side again.

▶PUSH

14

Your body should have two clear crease marks from steps 11 and 12: one mountain, one valley. Crease both so they also fold the other way.

15

Turn the creases into two inside reverse folds (see page 5). Push the top fold down inside the bottom one.

16

Flatten down the paper, then fold the top point over to the right.

17

Fold it the other way so it's also a mountain fold, then turn it into an inside reverse fold.

18

Fold the top right-hand point back to the left to form the crest.

19

Fold it the other way, so it's also a mountain fold, then turn it into an outside reverse fold.

20

Your paper should look like this. Fetch the other piece of paper.

21

Place your pieces of paper one on top of the other like this. Dab a bit of glue in the marked area. Turn the paper over and do the same on the other side.

22

Fold the dinosaur's legs down over the body.

23

Hold the paper in place for a minute. Once you let go, the paper should be stuck, which means your dino is ready to start calling out to its friends.

FINISHED!

TRICERATOPS

Say "Try-SER-ah-tops"

One of most famous dinosaurs, Triceratops is easy to recognize because of the three sharp horns on its head (its name means "Three-Horned-Face"). You'll be making this dinosaur in two parts, starting with the tail.

TAIL AND BACK LEGS

1

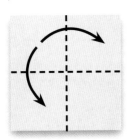

Place your paper like this, white side up with a straight edge facing you. Valley fold in half from top to bottom, and unfold. Then valley fold in half from left to right, and unfold.

2

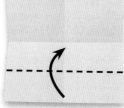

Fold the bottom edge up to the central crease.

3

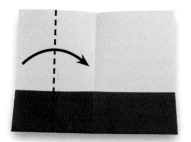

Fold the left edge over to the central crease.

4

Fold the right edge over to the central crease.

5

Fold the top left-hand corner over and down to the central crease.

6

Fold the top right-hand corner over to the central crease.

UNFOLD

7

Open up the fold you made in step 5.

8

Bring the top central point of the fold down to form a pocket. Then flatten it down to form a triangle shape.

★ ★ ★
HARD

9

Your paper should look like this. Repeat steps 7 and 8 on the right-hand side.

10

Fold the top point down, as shown.

UNFOLD

11 Unfold the fold you made in step 10.

UNFOLD

12 Fold the top point over to the right so it meets the crease you made in step 10.

UNFOLD

13 Unfold the fold you made in step 12.

14

Now fold the top point over to the left. Again, make sure it touches the crease you made in step 10.

15

Fold the left-hand central point up and to the left.

65

16 Repeat step 15 on the right-hand side.

17 Make a fold on the left-hand side, as shown.

18 Repeat step 17 on the right-hand side.

UNFOLD

19 Unfold the fold you made in step 17.

20 Bring the left-hand point of the upper layer over to the right.

PUSH

FLATTEN

21 As you bring the point across, push the paper in as shown to make a new fold and then flatten the paper down.

22 Your paper should look like this. Repeat steps 19 to 21 on the right-hand side.

OPEN

23 Open up the paper on the bottom left-hand side.

24

Lift the central point up and over to the left, so that the paper forms a triangle shape.

25

Flatten the paper down.

FLATTEN

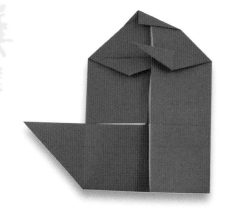

26

Your paper should look like this. Repeat steps 23 to 25 on the right-hand side.

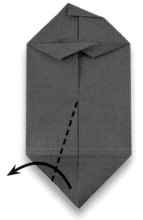

27

Fold the left hand point down and to the right.

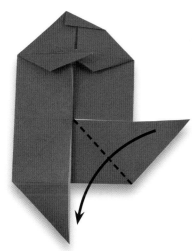

28

Fold the right-hand point down and to the left.

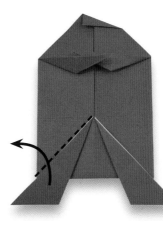

29

Fold the bottom left-hand point up and to the left, as shown.

30

Fold the bottom right-hand point up and to the right.

31

Fold the flap you made in step 29 over along its left edge.

32

Now fold the flap you mad in step 30 over along its right edge.

TURN OVER

33

Your paper should look like this. Turn it over from left to right.

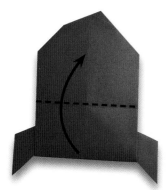

34

Fold the bottom edge of the paper up, as shown.

TURN OVER

35

Turn your paper back over from right to left.

36

Your legs are complete. Put them to one side while you get on with the head and front legs.

HEAD AND FRONT LEGS

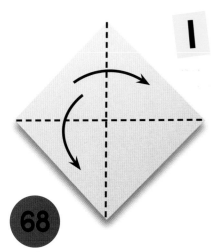

1

Take the second piece of paper and position it like this, white side up with a corner facing you. Fold it in half from top to bottom, and unfold. Then valley fold it in half from left to right, and unfold.

2

Fold the left-hand point and the right-hand point to the central line.

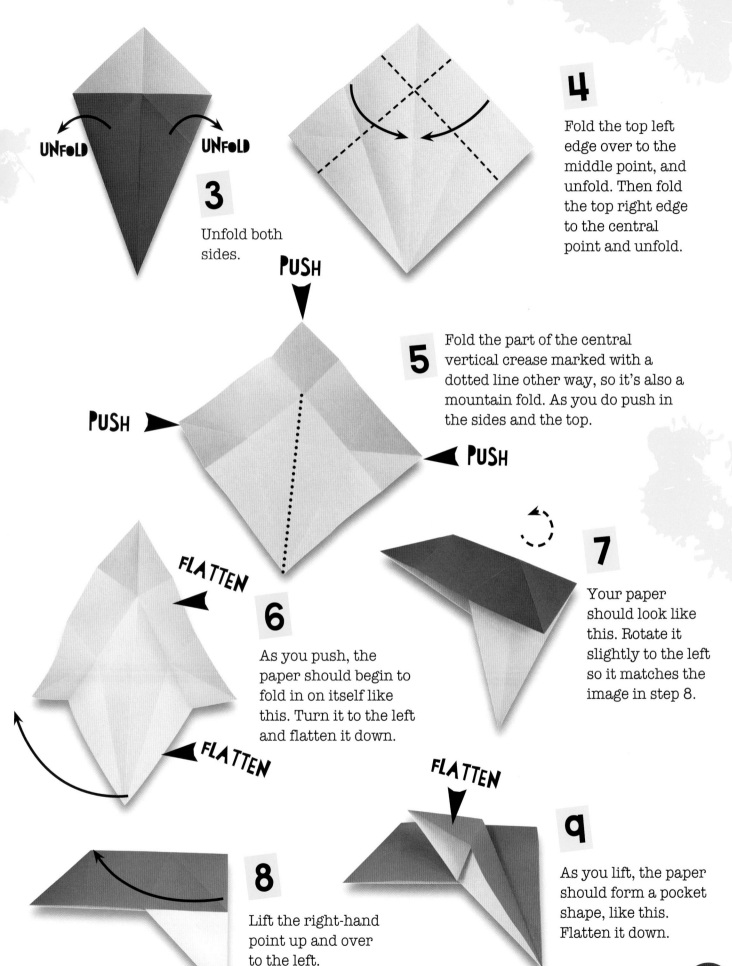

UNFOLD **UNFOLD**

3

Unfold both sides.

4

Fold the top left edge over to the middle point, and unfold. Then fold the top right edge to the central point and unfold.

PUSH

PUSH

PUSH

5

Fold the part of the central vertical crease marked with a dotted line other way, so it's also a mountain fold. As you do push in the sides and the top.

FLATTEN

6

As you push, the paper should begin to fold in on itself like this. Turn it to the left and flatten it down.

FLATTEN

7

Your paper should look like this. Rotate it slightly to the left so it matches the image in step 8.

8

Lift the right-hand point up and over to the left.

FLATTEN

9

As you lift, the paper should form a pocket shape, like this. Flatten it down.

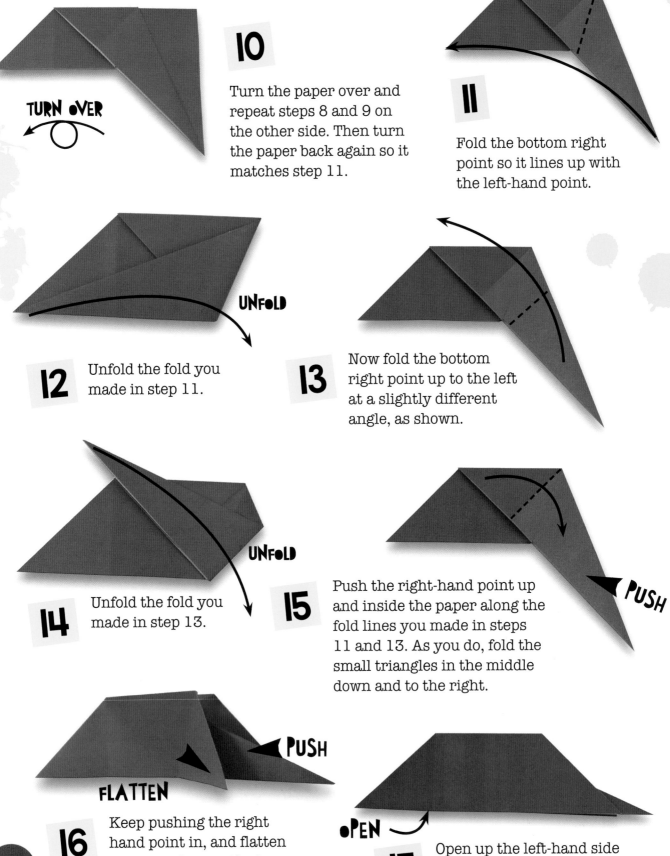

10

Turn the paper over and repeat steps 8 and 9 on the other side. Then turn the paper back again so it matches step 11.

TURN OVER

11

Fold the bottom right point so it lines up with the left-hand point.

UNFOLD

12 Unfold the fold you made in step 11.

13 Now fold the bottom right point up to the left at a slightly different angle, as shown.

UNFOLD

14 Unfold the fold you made in step 13.

15 Push the right-hand point up and inside the paper along the fold lines you made in steps 11 and 13. As you do, fold the small triangles in the middle down and to the right.

PUSH

PUSH

FLATTEN

16 Keep pushing the right hand point in, and flatten the triangle over the top.

OPEN

17 Open up the left-hand side so it forms a pocket.

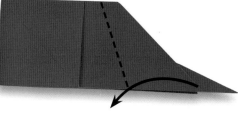

FLATTEN

18 Lift the middle point of the pocket up and to the right.

19 Flatten the paper down so it forms a square shape.

21 Turn your paper over and repeat step 20 on the other side. Then turn your paper back again.

20 Make a fold on the right-hand side as shown.

TURN OVER

22 Now take the first piece of paper. Fold it in half and then unfold.

23 Dab some glue in the areas shown. Start to fold your paper in half again.

24 Place the first piece of paper over the second piece of paper and hold in place.

25 Once the glue has dried, you've got one terrifying Triceratops. Charge!

FINISHED!

ARGENTINOSAURUS

Say "ar-jen-TEE-noh-SAW-rus"

This enormous, long-necked dino was named after the country in which it was found—Argentina. You'll make the tail and back legs first.

TAIL AND BACK LEGS

1 Start with your paper like this, white side up with a corner facing you. Valley fold it in half from top to bottom, and unfold. Then valley fold it in half from left to right, and unfold.

2 Fold the left- and right-hand points over to the central crease.

3 Fold the bottom point up to the top.

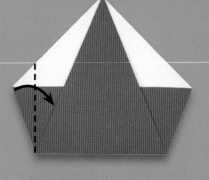

4 Fold the lower left edge across so it sits flush against the central triangle.

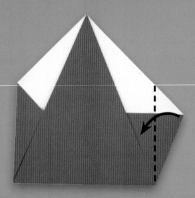

5 Repeat step 2 on the right-hand side.

UNFOLD

UNFOLD

UNFOLD

6 Unfold the folds you made in steps 3 to 5.

LIFT

7 Lift the central left point and move it down and to the right, as shown.

FLATTEN

8 Flatten the point down to form a triangle shape that goes over the central crease.

q Your paper should look like this. Repeat steps 7 and 8 on the right-hand side.

10 Fold down the top point, as shown, so it lines up with the flaps made in steps 7 to 9.

11 Mountain fold the paper in half from right to left.

12 Your paper should look this. Put it to one side while you make the head and front legs.

73

1

Take your other piece of paper and repeat steps 1 to 9 from the tail and back legs section, so it looks like this. Now rotate the paper 180°.

180°

2

Mountain fold the paper in half from right to left.

3

Fold the top point down and to the left as shown.

4

Fold it the other way so it's also a mountain fold, then unfold.

5

Make a new fold at a slightly different angle, as shown.

6

Fold it the other way so it's also a mountain fold, then unfold.

7

Push the top down so that the folds you made in steps 3 to 6 fold in on themselves, forming a step fold.

PUSH

8

Flatten the
paper down.

FLATTEN

9 Fold the top point
over to the right,
as shown.

10

Fold it the other
way so it's also
a mountain fold,
then turn it into an
outside reverse fold
(see page 5). This is
the head.

11

Your paper should
look like this. Rotate
it 90° to the right.

90°

12

Now bring back the
first piece of paper
and place it below
the second one,
like this.

13

Carefully push the second piece of paper
so that the white triangle goes inside the
first piece of paper while the legs go on
the outside.

PUSH

14

Keep pushing until the two
pieces of paper fit neatly
together.

15

Lift it up carefully and your
giant dino should be able
to stand upright.

FINISHED!

STEGOSAURUS

Say "STEG-oh-SAW-rus"

This great big dino had a brain about the size of a walnut—so it probably wasn't very bright. Use two different types of paper to really make the plates on its back stand out.

HEAD AND BODY

1 Let's make the body and head first. Start with your paper like this, white side up with a flat edge facing you. Valley fold it in half from left to right, then unfold.

2 Fold the right-hand edge over to the central crease.

3 Fold the left-hand edge over to the central crease.

4 Fold the top-right point down to the central crease, as shown.

5 Repeat step 4 with the other three corners.

6 Unfold the folds you made in steps 4 and 5.

UNFOLD   UNFOLD

UNFOLD   UNFOLD

 **PUSH**

7 Open out the top right corner, and push the right edge down and to the left, so the crease folds the other way, as in the image for step 8.

 **◄ FLATTEN**

8 Flatten the paper down.

★★ **MEDIUM**

9 Your paper should look like this. Repeat steps 7 and 8 with the other three corners.

10 Fold the top-right point of the upper layer down and to the left, as shown.

11 Fold the top left point down and to the right. It will go over the fold you made in step 10.

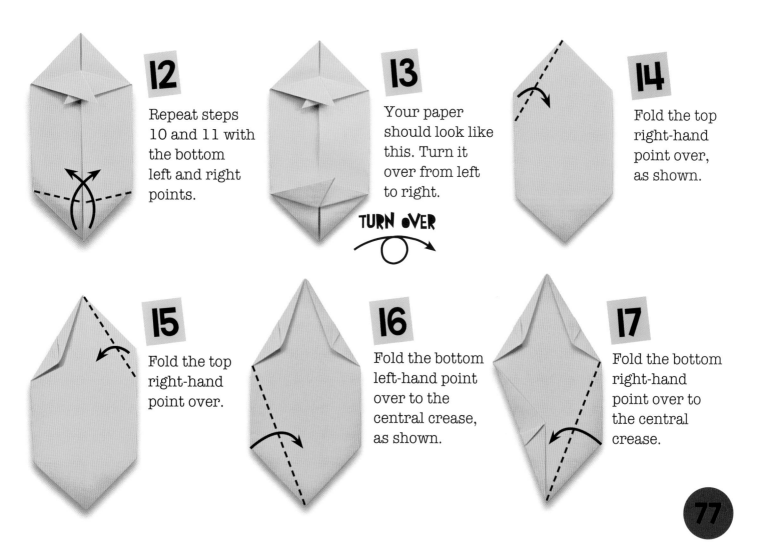

12 Repeat steps 10 and 11 with the bottom left and right points.

13 Your paper should look like this. Turn it over from left to right.

TURN OVER

14 Fold the top right-hand point over, as shown.

15 Fold the top right-hand point over.

16 Fold the bottom left-hand point over to the central crease, as shown.

17 Fold the bottom right-hand point over to the central crease.

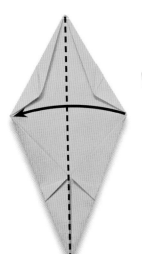

18

Your paper should look like this. Valley fold it in half from right to left.

19

Rotate the paper to the right.

90°

20

Mountain fold the left-hand point, as shown.

21

Fold it the other way, so it's also a valley fold, then turn it into an inside reverse fold (see page 5). This is the neck.

22

Make another mountain fold. Fold it the other way so it's also a valley fold, then turn it into an inside reverse fold. This is the head.

TUCK

23

Tuck the left hand point up into the head to form the snout.

24

Your paper should look like this. Put it to one side while you make the plates with the other piece of paper.

PLATES

1

Place your paper white side up with a straight edge facing you. Valley fold it in half from top to bottom, and unfold. Then valley fold it in half from left to right, and unfold.

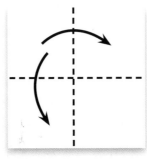

2

Fold the top right point down to the middle.

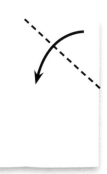

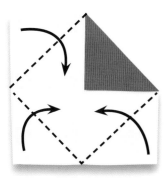

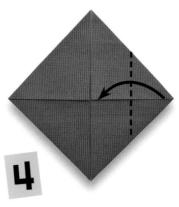

3 Repeat step 2 with the other three points.

4 Fold the right-hand point into the middle.

5 Repeat step 4 with the other three points.

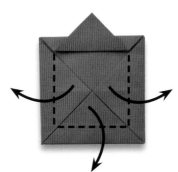

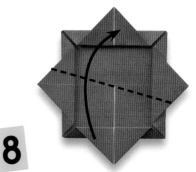

6 Fold the top point of the upper layer up, as shown.

7 Repeat step 6 with the other three points.

8 Fold the paper in half from bottom to top at a slight angle, as shown.

10 Slot the second piece of paper inside the first to complete your dino.

q Your paper should look like this. Fetch the first piece of paper.

II **Your spiky Stegosaurus is ready to take its first walk.**

FINISHED!

APATOSAURUS

Say "a-PAT-oh-SAW-rus"

From nose to tail, Apatosaurus was as long as a tennis court, making it one of the largest animals ever to walk the Earth. Your origami version will be a little smaller.

TURN OVER

1

Make a kite base (see page 6), but start with the white side facing down, so your paper looks like this. Rotate it 90° to the left.

2

Turn the paper over from top to bottom.

3

Fold the bottom point up to the central crease.

4

Fold the top point down to the central crease.

5

Unfold the lowest layer on both sides so that your paper matches the image in step 6.

6

Fold the bottom point up to the middle along the crease line, turning it from a mountain fold to a valley fold.

7 Repeat step 6 with the top point.

8 On the lower half, lift the point of the top flap and bring it over to the right so it begins to form a triangle shape, as in the image in step 9.

FLATTEN

9 Flatten the paper down.

10 Your paper should look like this. Repeat steps 8 and 9 on the top half.

11 Fold the bottom left point up to the central crease.

12 Repeat step 11 at the top of the paper.

OPEN

13 Open up the fold you made in step 11 and start bringing the lower point over to the right, as in image 14.

FLATTEN

14 Flatten the point down so it forms a triangle shape.

15 Repeat steps 13 and 14 at the top.

16 Your paper should look like this. Mountain fold it in half from bottom to top.

OPEN

17 Pull out the points to form the feet. Do the same on the other side.

APATOSAURUS CONTINUED...

18 Fold the right-hand point up, as shown.

19 Fold it the other way so it's also a mountain fold, then turn it into an inside reverse fold (see page 5).

20 Your paper should look like this. Fold the top right-hand point back to the left to start forming the head.

21 Fold it the other way so it's also a mountain fold. Then turn it into an inside reverse fold. This is the head.

22 Fold the upper layer of the head down, as shown to create a flat shape.

23 Mountain fold the right-hand point over, as shown, to form the snout.

24

Make sure the legs are standing straight out from the body and your Apatosaurus should be able to stand up. Doesn't he look fierce!

FINISHED!

SEA AND SKY

When dinosaurs roamed the Earth, other strange reptiles swam in the seas and soared through the clouds. The following pages will show you how to make some of these bizarre beasts.

QUETZALCOATLUS

Say "KWET-zal-koh-AT-luss"

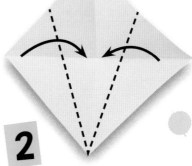

This giant flying dinosaur is easier to make than it is to say. You'll need scissors to complete this project—cut carefully when you make its crest.

1

Place your paper like this, white side up with a corner facing you. Fold in half from left to right, and unfold. Then fold in half from top to bottom, and unfold.

2

Fold the left and right points to the central crease, as shown.

3

Your paper should look like this. Turn it over from left to right.

TURN OVER

4

Make a large step fold, as shown (see page 4).

5

Your paper should look like this. Mountain fold it in half from right to left.

6

Now rotate your paper 90° to the right.

90°

7 Fold the left-hand point up and to the left, as shown.

8 Fold it the other way, so it's also a mountain fold, and then turn it into an inside reverse fold (see page 5).

9 Mountain fold the top left-hand point over to the left. This is the head.

10 Fold the head down, as shown.

11 Use your scissors to make two small cuts behind the head, as shown.

12 Open up the wings of your creation.

13 Add eyes and a mouth and your flying reptile is complete.

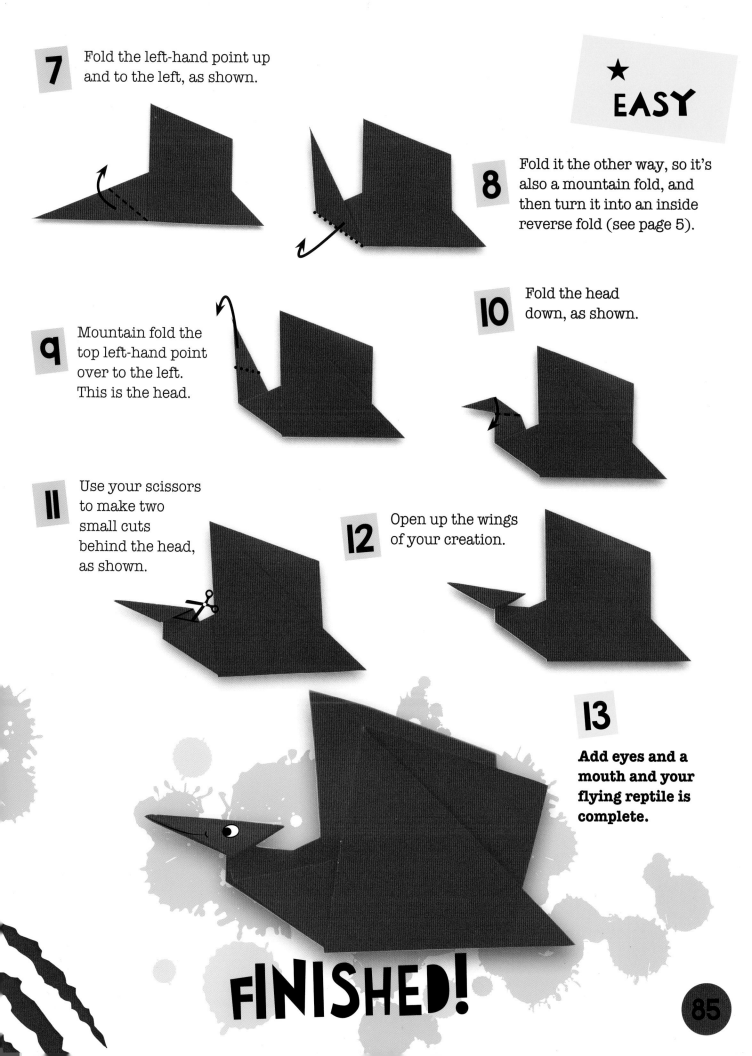

FINISHED!

85

PLIOSAURUS

Say "PLY-oh-SAW-rus"

This fierce-looking creature wasn't a dinosaur—although it looked a lot like one. It was a reptile that lived in the sea. You'll need two pieces of paper for this project: one for the body and one for the legs.

BODY

1 Let's start with the Pliosaurus' body. Place your paper white side up with a corner facing you. Valley fold in half from left to right, and unfold.

2 Fold the bottom right edge over to the top left edge, as shown, then unfold.

3 Fold the right-hand point over to crease you made in step 2.

4 Fold the top left-hand edge over so it meets up with the fold you made in step 3.

5 Fold the top point down to the bottom point.

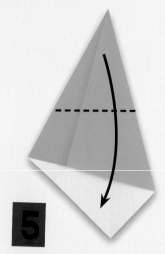

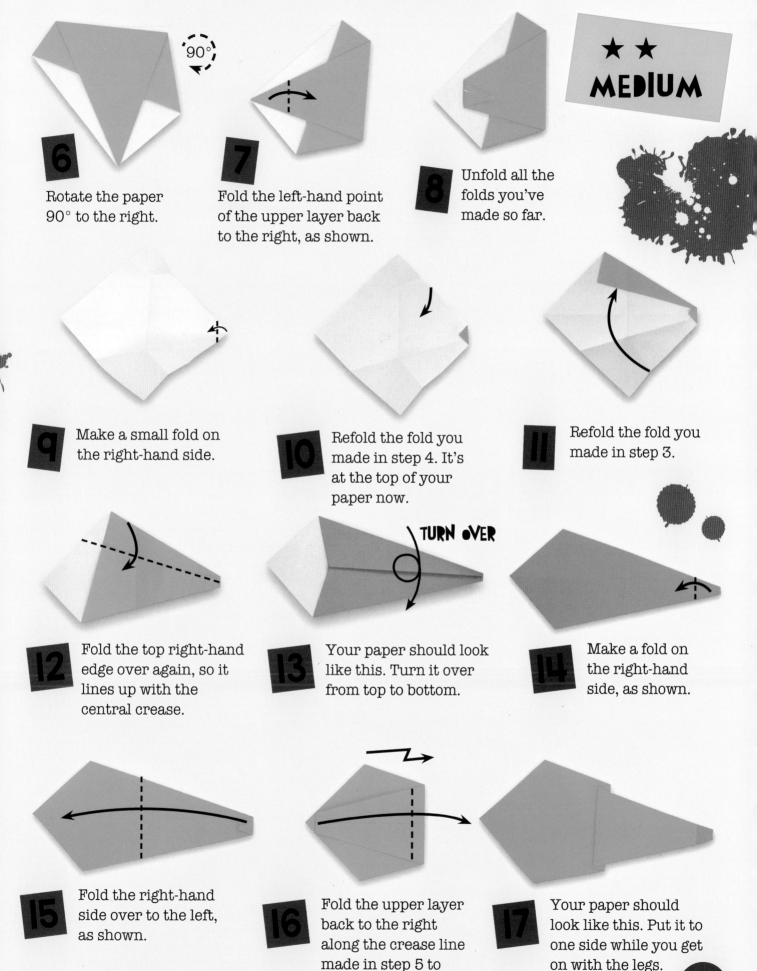

6 Rotate the paper 90° to the right.

7 Fold the left-hand point of the upper layer back to the right, as shown.

8 Unfold all the folds you've made so far.

9 Make a small fold on the right-hand side.

10 Refold the fold you made in step 4. It's at the top of your paper now.

11 Refold the fold you made in step 3.

12 Fold the top right-hand edge over again, so it lines up with the central crease.

13 Your paper should look like this. Turn it over from top to bottom.

TURN OVER

14 Make a fold on the right-hand side, as shown.

15 Fold the right-hand side over to the left, as shown.

16 Fold the upper layer back to the right along the crease line made in step 5 to form a step fold.

17 Your paper should look like this. Put it to one side while you get on with the legs.

1 Place your paper like this, white side up with a corner facing you. Fold in half from left to right, and unfold. Then fold in half from top to bottom, and unfold.

2 Turn the paper so a straight edge is facing you. Now fold in half from left to right, and unfold. Then fold in half from top to bottom, and unfold.

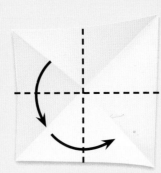

TURN OVER

3 Your paper should look like this. Turn it over from left to right.

4 Fold the bottom right-hand corner up to the central point.

5 Repeat step 4 with the other three corners.

UNFOLD UNFOLD

UNFOLD UNFOLD

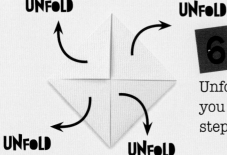

6 Unfold the folds you made in steps 4 and 5.

7 Turn the paper over from left to right.

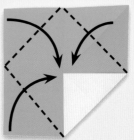

TURN OVER

OPEN

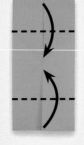

8 Fold the left- and right-hand edges to the central crease.

9 Fold the top and bottom edges to the central crease.

10 Open up the paper in the top left corner. Take the central point of the second layer and bring it over to the left so it forms a triangle shape, as in the image for step 11.

11 Your paper should look like this. Repeat step 10 on the right side.

12 Repeat steps 10 and 11 on the bottom half of the paper.

13 Fold the top left-hand point up and to the right, as shown.

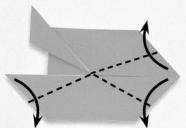

14 Repeat step 13 on the other three sides.

15 Your paper should look like this. Fetch the first piece of paper. It's time to put your Pliosaurus together.

16 Place your pieces of paper like this. Slide the legs over the body. Tuck the paper under the step fold made in step 16 of the Body stage.

17 Mountain fold over the points at the top and bottom, as shown.

18 Start mountain folding your paper in half from top to bottom.

19 As you fold, tuck the right-hand end over to form the snout.

20 Add a fearsome set of teeth, some large eyes and then release your new origami monster.

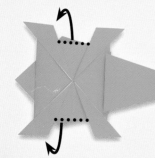

FINISHED!

ICHTHYOSAURUS

Say "ICK-thee-oh-SAW-rus"

Ichthyosaurs looked quite a lot like modern dolphins. They swam fast through the oceans looking for fish to eat.

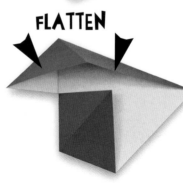

1

Place your paper like this, white side up with a corner facing you. Valley fold in half from top to bottom, and unfold. Then valley fold in half from left to right, and unfold.

2

Fold the top corner down to the central crease.

3

Fold the bottom corner up to the central crease.

4

Your paper should look like this. Turn it over from top to bottom.

TURN OVER

5

Fold the paper in half from left to right.

6

Open up the fold on the top left-hand side, and bring the point of this flap over to the left.

7

FLATTEN

The fold you opened in step 7 should begin to form a triangle shape, like this. Flatten it down.

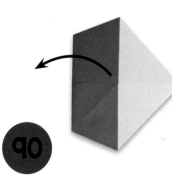

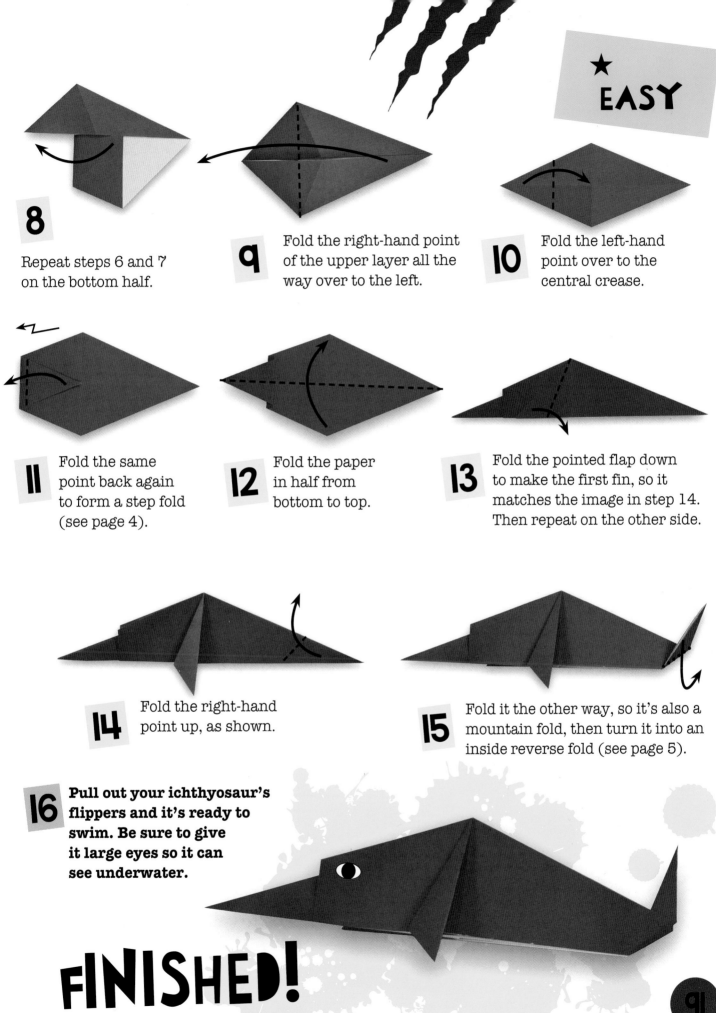

8 Repeat steps 6 and 7 on the bottom half.

9 Fold the right-hand point of the upper layer all the way over to the left.

10 Fold the left-hand point over to the central crease.

11 Fold the same point back again to form a step fold (see page 4).

12 Fold the paper in half from bottom to top.

13 Fold the pointed flap down to make the first fin, so it matches the image in step 14. Then repeat on the other side.

14 Fold the right-hand point up, as shown.

15 Fold it the other way, so it's also a mountain fold, then turn it into an inside reverse fold (see page 5).

16 Pull out your ichthyosaur's flippers and it's ready to swim. Be sure to give it large eyes so it can see underwater.

FINISHED!

ELASMOSAURUS

Say "ee-LAZ-moh-SAW-rus"

Although it lived in the sea, this long-necked creature had to swim to the surface to breathe. It also laid its eggs on land, much like turtles do today.

START WITH A FISH BASE

1 Start with a fish base, like this (see page 6). Rotate your paper 90° to the right.

90°

2 Mountain fold the paper in half from bottom to top.

3 Fold the pointed flap down and to the right to form the first fin. Repeat on the other side to make the other fin.

4 Fold the left-hand point up and to the right, as shown.

5 Fold it the other way, so it's also a mountain fold, then turn it into an inside reverse fold (see page 5).

6 Mountain fold over the left-hand point of the upper layer.

7 Do the same on the other side.

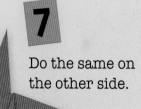

8 Valley fold the top point over to the left.

9 Fold it the other way so it's also a mountain fold, then turn it into an inside reverse fold (see page 5). This is the head.

10 Fold and flatten down the upper layer of the head so it matches the image in step 11.

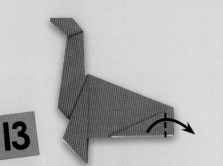

11 Mountain fold the top left point to form the snout.

12 Fold the right-hand point back to the left. Then fold it the other way so it's also a mountain fold.

13 Make another valley fold, back to the right, as shown. Again, fold it the other way so it's also a mountain fold.

14 Turn the folds you made in steps 12 and 13 into two inside reverse folds, one inside the other.

15 Valley fold the bottom point up to create the first flipper.

16 Do the same on the other side to create the other flipper.

17 Spread the flippers out and your Elasmosaurus should be able to stand up and waddle its way down to the shore.

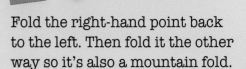

FINISHED!

91

PTERANODON

Say "teh-RAN-oh-don"

Pteranodon had a distinctive crest on its head, and used its large leathery wings to soar through the prehistoric skies. Here's how to make your own origami version.

1 Fold the paper in half from left to right, then unfold.

2 Fold the paper in half from top to bottom.

3 Fold the left-hand point up and to the right to meet the central crease.

4 Repeat step 3 on the right-hand side.

5 Your paper should look like this. Fold the top left point down and to the left, as shown.

6 Repeat step 5 on the right-hand side.

7 OPEN ••• OPEN
Open out the paper at the bottom and lift up the bottom point of the upper layer a little way, so it sits front of the other layers.

94

TUCK BEHIND ► ◄ TUCK BEHIND

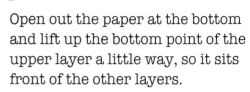

8 As you lift, the white triangles at the top of the paper should tuck behind the central triangle. Flatten your paper down.

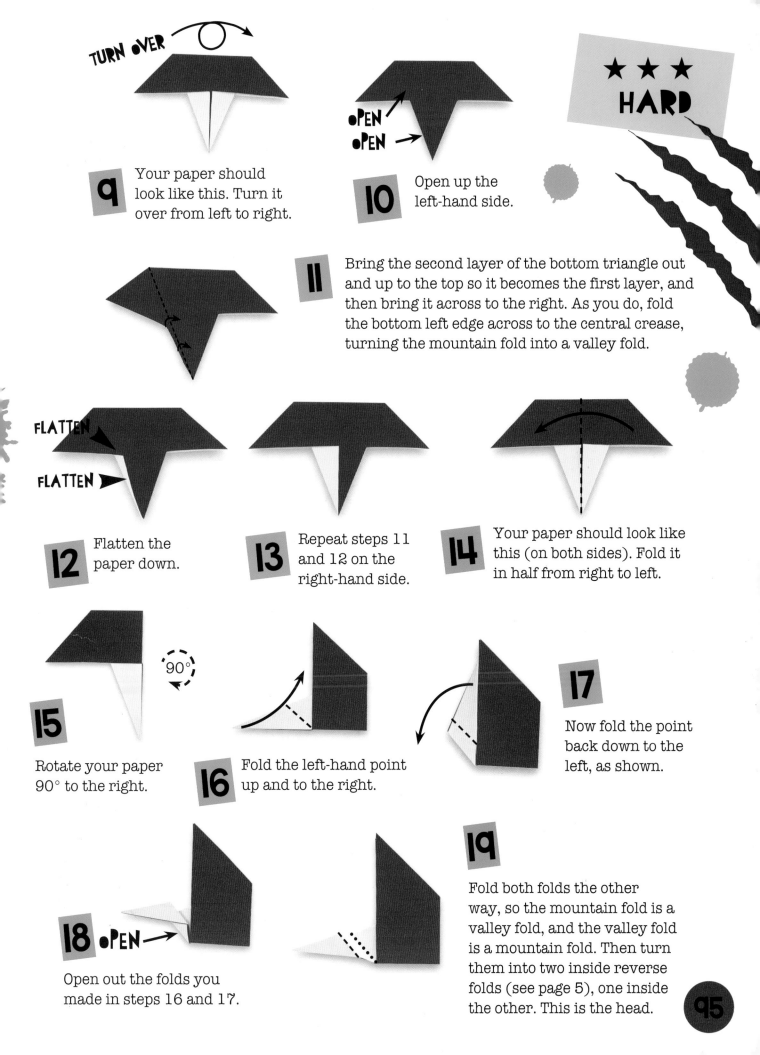

TURN OVER

★ ★ ★
HARD

9 Your paper should look like this. Turn it over from left to right.

10 Open up the left-hand side.

OPEN
OPEN

11 Bring the second layer of the bottom triangle out and up to the top so it becomes the first layer, and then bring it across to the right. As you do, fold the bottom left edge across to the central crease, turning the mountain fold into a valley fold.

FLATTEN

FLATTEN

12 Flatten the paper down.

13 Repeat steps 11 and 12 on the right-hand side.

14 Your paper should look like this (on both sides). Fold it in half from right to left.

15 Rotate your paper 90° to the right.

90°

16 Fold the left-hand point up and to the right.

17 Now fold the point back down to the left, as shown.

18 OPEN Open out the folds you made in steps 16 and 17.

19 Fold both folds the other way, so the mountain fold is a valley fold, and the valley fold is a mountain fold. Then turn them into two inside reverse folds (see page 5), one inside the other. This is the head.

95

PULL

20

Pull back the top layer of the head.

21

Make a valley fold as shown.

22

Fold it the other way so it's also a mountain fold, then turn it into an outside reverse fold (see page 5). This is the crest.

FLATTEN

23

Flatten the paper down, and tuck the head between the wings.

24

Fold down the top wing, as shown.

25

Now fold down the other wing, so it matches the first.

26

Your paper should look like this.

27

Spread your Pteranodon's wings out, and it's ready to take to the skies.

FINISHED!